"*The Day I Met God* may be the mo_____ this year! I was inspired, delighted, and in tears over some of the drama and the triumphs. For those of faith, it will encourage you; for those seeking answers, they're in the pages of this book. Don't miss this one!"

BERT DECKER, FOUNDER, DECKER COMMUNICATIONS;
AUTHOR, *Speaking With Bold Assurance*

"Wow! These are exciting and compelling. God can do anything! This is inspiring material."

RALPH WINTER, EXECUTIVE PRODUCER,
Star Trek IV AND *Planet of the Apes*

"Ordinary people encounter the extraordinary in this moving collection of stories. *The Day I Met God* provides a window into mankind's ongoing search for a meaningful life."

DARCY RICE, NOVELIST, PLAYWRIGHT, AND FREELANCE WRITER

"A fascinating book that stays with you. I won't soon forget the private, life-changing moments that the famous and the *Everyman* have shared in these pages. Nothing is more engrossing than real people telling the truth. *The Day I Met God* is for anyone who has ever considered himself to be on a 'spiritual journey.' Whether or not you have already met God, you will most certainly meet Him here."

MARTHA WILLIAMSON, EXECUTIVE PRODUCER, *Touched by an Angel*

"Finding God has never been easy, but it's even less so in our fast-moving society. In the rush to live, we rarely slow down enough to consider *why* we live the way we do. But if you've ever experienced the feeling that there is something deeper in life, something beyond mere existence, something that suggests more permanence than the latest fad, fashion, or fun, this book is a must-read. These stories show how others have felt the same thing and have pursued their quest to find out what, or Who, was drawing them."

MARK T. CLARK, PH.D., PROFESSOR AND CHAIRMAN OF POLITICAL SCIENCE
CALIFORNIA STATE UNIVERSITY, SAN BERNARDINO

"Karen and Jim Covell and Victorya Michaels Rogers have done a wonderful job of bringing together a diverse collection of inspiring stories of how God broke into the lives of ordinary people—often in extraordinary ways! I heartily recommend this book to any seeker or believer who wants to be energized in his or her own walk with God."

DAVID J. BROBECK JR., ATTORNEY AT LAW

The day I Met God

EXTRAORDINARY STORIES OF LIFE-CHANGING MIRACLES

Jim & Karen Covell

Victorya Michaels Rogers

Multnomah Publishers · Sisters, Oregon

THE DAY I MET GOD
published by Multnomah Publishers, Inc.

© 2001 by Jim Covell, Karen Covell, and Victorya Michaels Rogers

International Standard Book Number: 1-57673-786-1

Cover design by Christopher Gilbert/Uttley DouPonce DesignWorks
Cover photo by Photonica

Scripture quotations are from:
The Holy Bible, New International Version © 1973, 1984 by International Bible
Society, used by permission of Zondervan Publishing House

Multnomah is a trademark of Multnomah Publishers, Inc., and is registered
in the U.S. Patent and Trademark Office.
The colophon is a trademark of Multnomah Publishers, Inc.

Printed in the United States of America

For information:

MULTNOMAH PUBLISHERS, INC.•POST OFFICE BOX 1720•SISTERS, OREGON 97759

Library of Congress Cataloging-in-Publication Data:
Covell, Jim.
    The day I met God : extraordinary stories of life-changing miracles /
by Jim and Karen Covell and Victorya Michaels Rogers.
        p. cm.
    ISBN 1-57673-786-1 (pbk.)
    1. Life change events–Religious aspects–Christianity. 2. Conversion–
Christianity. I. Covell, Karen. II. Rogers, Victorya Michaels. III. Title.
    BV4908.5 .C68 2001
    248.2'4'0922–dc21

                            2001001028

01 02 03 04 05—10 9 8 7 6 5 4 3 2 1

We dedicate this book to our parents,

Jim and LaJuan Covell,
Joe and Jane Zarish, and
Curtis and Sandra Sterud,

who first introduced each one of us to God.

TABLE OF CONTENTS

ACKNOWLEDGMENTS

All three of us want to thank each and every one of you who opened up your lives to us and risked telling us the most personal details of your spiritual journeys—just so that you could encourage others. We couldn't have done this without you. Whether your story was included in this volume or not, you have touched us and led us into a richer intimacy with God. Thank you.

We also thank Bill Jensen and Penny Whipps for continuing to believe in us and John Bollow and our great moms—Jane, LaJuan, Pat, and Sandra—for helping us edit and edit again. Thanks to one another: Three strands truly are stronger than one. But most of all, thanks to our angel, Judith St. Pierre, who is a supporter, friend, and editor extraordinaire!

Soli Deo Gloria.

Preface

Since time began, man has asked: Does God care about us? Does He perform miracles? Can we meet Him? Man's search for a tangible God goes on.

In *Les Miserables,* Jean Valjean said, "To love another person is to see the face of God." Some people have seen God in the face of a newborn child; some, the blinding light of His face on their deathbeds. Moses said that he saw God in a burning bush. God has spoken to some people in a still, small voice, while He has revealed Himself to others in vivid dreams or detailed visions. Even Woody Allen said, "If only God would give me some clear sign! Like making a large deposit in my name at a Swiss bank...."

The stories in this book have one thing in common: The people who wrote them have all met God in a personal way. As snowflakes, stars, and grains of sand differ vastly from one another, so do the experiences of every person who has met God. No two stories are alike. Some are amazing; some are tragic; some are simply touching—but all are extraordinary.

These stories are not told in full. We live in a world where people's lives are reduced to sixty-minute television dramas, thirty-minute sitcoms, and ten-second sound bytes. Still, we hope that even in these abbreviated versions you will get a vivid sense of the power and the miracle behind the events they describe. The day they met God, all of these people were changed in positive, empowering ways that added hope, joy, and love to their once empty, unfulfilled, or broken lives.

Does God care about us? Does He perform miracles? Can we meet Him?

Read these stories and find out!

Jim, Karen, and Victorya

1

A Family for Johnny

Johnny Lee Clary

*One man cannot hold another man down in the ditch
without remaining down in the ditch with him.*
BOOKER T. WASHINGTON

I learned how to hate early in life. When I was five years old, my father encouraged me to lean out our car window and shout racial slurs as blacks came out of the supermarket. Daddy grinned and patted me on the back. "That's my boy," he said.

My mother was an alcoholic who never gave me any attention. So I hung out with Dad, hunting and fishing. When I was older, I would sit up late at night listening to my Uncle Harold talk about shooting at black men who crossed his property. Daddy and Uncle Harold would howl with laughter.

My grandmother, though, read the Bible to me, took me to Sunday school, and told me that she was praying for me. One Sunday I came home singing a song I had learned: "Jesus loves the little children—all the children of the world. Red and yellow, black and white, they are precious in His sight. Jesus loves the little children of the world."

"Don't ever let me catch you singing words like that again!" Daddy thundered.

That was the end of Sunday school and learning about Jesus, so I began looking for someone else to worship, like Bonnie and Clyde, John Dillinger, Pretty Boy Floyd, Machine Gun Kelly, and Al Capone. Gangsters fascinated me, and since very few things seemed to please my daddy, studying them was one of the few things that got me his approval.

One night when I was eleven, I came home and found my Daddy standing in the middle of his room holding a gun to his head. I watched in horror as he pulled the trigger—right in front of me.

Son, what you need is a real family— the Klan. Come join us, and we'll look after you.

After the funeral, while I was still in shock, Mama sent me to California to live with my older sister and her ex-con boyfriend. My sister tolerated me only for the government check, and she let her boyfriend beat me and call me horrible names. Lonely and confused, I started drinking. I spent most of my time either hanging out in the streets until I passed out drunk or just lying on my sister's old sofa staring at the TV.

One day, I watched a talk-show host interview David Duke, the Grand Wizard of the Ku Klux Klan. Fascinated by Duke, I asked around to find out how I could get in touch with the Klan, and before long a representative, Bob, came to visit. After we talked for a while, he said, "Son, what you need is a real family— the Klan. Come join us, and we'll look after you. I think you'll even be a leader someday."

That was all I needed to hear. I desperately needed some place to belong, and these people were the first "family" I had had who cared about me. Week after week, Bob took me to meetings and then brought me home. At the age of fourteen, I became a full-fledged member of the Klan and part of a family—David Duke's family.

Eventually, I became Duke's bodyguard. As a more intimate member of the family, I quickly saw what a hypocrite Duke was and that his klan wasn't a family at all. So I decided to join a rival klan headed by Bill Wilkinson, Duke's arch rival.

I moved up in the ranks in no time. I became a tireless recruiter for the Klan in Oklahoma, and it grew under my leadership. I was a fiery and effective speaker as I spread the gospel of hate. I started two programs: one to recruit members straight out of police departments and another called Youth Core to sign up high school students. Both programs flourished. As the membership grew, so did my power and prestige, and by the time I was twenty, I was the Grand Dragon of Oklahoma.

We knew the power of the media and took every chance we got to use it to boost our recruitment. When I appeared on the Morton Downey Jr. show, my opening statement was "White Power!"—accompanied by a kind of Heil-Hitler, raised-arm salute. I was kicked off the show before I got a chance to say another word, but I took it as victory for our side because any media exposure was a coup for us. Bad press was much better than no press at all.

That's why, when I was asked to speak on a Tulsa radio station in 1979, I jumped at the chance. Only shortly before the program did I learn that I was to debate Reverend Wade Watts, a local leader of the NAACP. But I wasn't worried. I looked forward to a chance to put a black man in his place—especially a leader of the NAACP!

I began by refusing to shake hands with Reverend Watts, a nicely dressed, older black preacher who was carrying a worn Bible and wearing a smile on his strong, kind face. In a dignified manner, he looked straight into my eyes, reached out and took my hand, and shook it anyway.

"Hello, Mr. Clary," he said. "I'm Reverend Watts. Before we go in, I just want you to know that I love you and Jesus loves you." I couldn't believe he dared say that to me. I pulled my hand away and headed toward the studio.

Our debate went back and forth. I fired off reasons the races should never have anything to do with each other; the reverend quoted Scripture and politely refuted everything I said. When he zeroed in on me with pointed questions about my beliefs, I could only mumble the generic slogans of the Klan. His calm, gentle attitude angered and flustered me. I couldn't come back at him with anything fresh or original. I became so uncomfortable that I finally snarled, "I'm not listening to any more of this" and stormed out.

I grabbed my belongings and was heading through the lobby when the reverend calmly walked up to me. I was about to push him out of my way when I saw that he was holding a baby in his arms.

I was out to destroy his life. I would make him hate me— whatever it took.

"Mr. Clary, this is my daughter Tia," he said. "And I have one last question for you." He held out a little girl with shining dark eyes and skin. She was looking straight at me with one of the sweetest expressions I had ever seen. "You say you hate all black people, Mr. Clary. Just tell me—how can you hate this child?"

Stunned and speechless, I turned and almost ran toward the door. I heard the reverend call after me: "I'm going to love you and pray for you, Mr. Clary, whether you like it or not!"

I didn't like it. I hated it! Those words burned in my ears.

For ten years, I had two passionate goals. The first was to climb the Klan's national ranks to the position of Imperial Wizard, and the second was to make Reverend Wade Watts pay for what he had done. I was out to destroy his life. I would make him hate me— whatever it took.

The Oklahoma Klan waged a ferocious campaign against Reverend Watts. Klansmen barraged his family with threatening phone calls, broke his windows, and torched effigies on his lawn. We even set fire to his church. We harassed his thirteen children, and they had to be escorted to school by the highway patrol. Every once in a while I found myself thinking about that baby, little Tia. But my hate drove the thought away.

Still, nothing the Klan did stopped the reverend from working for justice and equality. We couldn't intimidate or scare him enough to shut him up. When he joined ranks with an Oklahoma senator to outlaw the telephone hot lines we used for recruiting, we called an emergency meeting. When the Klan gathered, I announced that I had decided to stop Watts once and for all—and I would do it myself! With Klan members crowded around me, I dialed his home.

"I want you to know we're coming to get you," I hissed when the reverend answered. "And this time we mean business!"

"Hello, Johnny Lee!" he said, as though hearing from a long-lost relative. "You don't have to come for me; I'll meet you. How about at a nice little restaurant I know out on Highway 270? I'm buying."

"This isn't a joke, old man. We're coming over, and when we're finished, you'll wish you'd never crossed us."

"That place has the best home cooking you ever tasted! Apple pie that'll make you long for more. Fluffy mashed potatoes. Iced tea in mason jars...."

I slammed down the phone. "He wants to take us out to dinner," I said in disbelief. "Talked about apple pie and iced tea."

"The old man's gone crazy," someone said. "Let's forget about him."

We didn't. One day we surrounded him in that café. He had a plate of chicken on the table in front of him. Everyone watched in silence as I strutted up to him and told him that we were going to do the same thing to him that he did to that chicken. You could have heard a pin drop. Calmly, Reverend Watts picked up the chicken—and kissed it. The entire café burst out laughing, and we left.

We left Reverend Watts alone after that. I turned my energies to solidifying my position in my "family," and in 1989 I was appointed Imperial Wizard. I had just gone through a divorce and lost custody of my baby daughter, and in desperation I focused on creating a new family. I wanted to unify all hate groups—from skinheads to neo-Nazis—under the umbrella of the Klan. Hoping they would unite under my leadership, I arranged a national meeting.

But on the day of the gathering, the Klan, skinheads, and neo-Nazis all started fighting, accusing one another of stealing their members and mailing lists. By the time I arrived, my unity meeting was in shambles. As I looked out over the stormy proceedings, I thought: *These groups want to "purify" the world and have it all be like them, but they hate one another. Their hate extends to all colors, backgrounds, and ages, even to babies like Reverend Wade Watts's little daughter Tia. Do I really want to live in a world of people like that? Are these the people I want to be my family?*

"How can you hate this child?" Reverend Watts had asked me. How far I had come from the days I had sung those words: "Jesus loves the little children—all the children of the world. Red and yellow, black and white, they are precious in His sight...."

Suddenly I was repulsed by the poison that swirled around me. I felt sick to my stomach. Confused thoughts whirled through my head. On my way to the meeting, police had beaten me up and impounded my car to try to stop me from getting there. And here we were beating each other up too. I turned in disgust and walked out the door.

From that point on, I started embarrassing members by turning up drunk at meetings. Finally I told the other Klan officials that I was giving up my position and leaving the group forever. They willingly allowed me to leave.

Then my life really fell apart. As the weeks passed, filled by a sense of shame and worthlessness, I fell into a deep depression. By this time I had lost a marriage, a child, and all my friends. I had no job, no identity, and no purpose. There was nothing left for me but the numbness of alcohol. So one day, alone in my shabby, dark apartment, I raised a loaded gun to my head. *Daddy, I'm following in your footsteps. There's no other way to go....*

Just as I was about to pull the trigger, sunlight broke through the partially closed blinds and fell on a Bible that lay gathering dust on my bookshelf. It was an old Bible like the one Reverend Watts had carried that day at the radio station—an old Bible like the one I had seen my grandmother read so many times.

Maybe there is another way. I put down the gun and picked up the Bible. It fell open to Luke 15—the Parable of the Prodigal Son, who was joyfully welcomed home by the father he had woefully wronged. I read the story three times and then fell on my knees and wept. That was the night I met God—or that He met me.

I quietly joined a church, a multiracial congregation. I kept a low profile, studying the Scriptures and getting grounded in God's truths and promises. For two years I couldn't get enough of Jesus. The hate in me gave way to hope, joy, and even love—something I had never before experienced. As impossible as it seemed at first, I was becoming a new person, from the inside out. At last, in 1991, I picked up the phone and placed a call I knew I had to make.

Mrs. Watts answered. Without identifying myself, I asked if Reverend Watts was there. It had been ten years since our last conversation, but she must have known my voice, for when the Reverend got on the line, his first words were: "This is that Ku Klux Klansman!" Then he said warmly, "Hello, Johnny Lee."

"Reverend Watts, I want you to know that I resigned from the KKK two years ago. I gave my heart to Jesus, and I'm a member of an interracial church."

"Praise the Lord!" he shouted. "I've never stopped praying for you! Would you do me the honor of speaking at my church?"

How can he forgive me? How could he have cared about me all those years? I hesitantly accepted, almost intimidated by the love that I knew I would find in his church.

Looking out over Reverend Watts's congregation of mostly black faces, I told my story simply, not hiding my past or sugarcoating the depth and ugliness of my involvement in the Klan. I told them that racism is a learned response but that love can be learned as well. Then I told them how God had miraculously changed all the hate in my heart to love and how I had discovered that I couldn't be a Christian and hate my brother.

I told them that racism is a learned response but that love can be learned as well.

There was silence when I finished. A teenage girl got to her feet and ran down the aisle toward me, arms open. I moved in front of the altar to pray with her. As I passed the reverend, I realized that he was weeping. "Don't you know who that is, Johnny Lee?" he asked quietly. "That's Tia. That's my baby."

All I had ever wanted was a family, and there had been one for me all along—waiting for me with open arms, in my own hometown.

Johnny Lee is founder of Johnny Lee Clary Ministries and Colorblind Operations, Inc., which offers healing from unforgivingness, hate, suicidal tendencies, and substance abuse. An ordained minister, he has appeared on television and radio programs all over the world. Since 1990, Johnny Lee has been a member of Victory Christian Center in Tulsa, Oklahoma, one of the nation's largest multiracial, interdenominational churches. Visit his web site at www.johnnyleeclary.com.

2

150 Days

Joseph Woodard

Life can only be understood backwards, but it must be lived forwards.
SØREN KIERKEGAARD

As a young child, I never thought about God at all. I did go to church, though. The local church had a bus, and on Sunday mornings the driver would come around our neighborhood to pick up kids who wanted to go to church. Riding the bus was exciting, and I really liked that bus driver. The moment my brother, Jimmy, and I heard the horn blowing, we ran out the door and hopped on the bus.

I didn't learn anything when I got to church, at least not that I remember. It was that bus driver who had the real impact on me. He gave us treats and extra rides around the block, and he always had a "dollar giveaway" for the child who sat in the "special" seat. I couldn't wait to guess which seat would get me the dollar.

When I was thirteen, my parents separated, and I was left without a dad. I was devastated, and during the two years that followed, my life completely fell apart. I felt like a failure. Taking care of two young sons was too much for my mother, who was deaf.

She tried her best, but we sometimes went without food and didn't get new clothes, let alone birthday or Christmas presents.

Only one positive thing happened during those two years. A local farmer heard about my family's situation and let Jimmy and me work on his farm to help meet our needs. Roy was a gentle bear, a loving man who also spent special time with us boys. He must have either felt sorry for us or just really loved us, because he poured his life into us. Ball games, dinner outings, and special events with him filled the gap left by our missing father. One Christmas, Roy even invited Jimmy and me to dinner, and there were presents under their tree for us. They were the only presents we got that year.

In showing me that someone really cared about and believed in me, Roy gave me a glimmer of hope and a reason to go on. Knowing him made me feel that I wasn't a complete failure after all. But just when I thought we were going to be okay, a large piece of farm equipment fell on him while he was working. At age thirty-nine, Roy was dead.

This tragedy prompted me to ask questions I had never asked before, such as "Where do we go after we die?" I turned to a couple of Christian leaders in my community for answers. They told me about Jesus and said that He would always take care of me, no matter which people were in or out of my life. For several years I learned as much about God as I could, and for the first time I felt hope. But I didn't make a life commitment to follow and obey Him, and as life got in the way, it didn't really last.

Five years later, in 1982, I got married. Sherry and I didn't attend church after our wedding day. We had two sons three years apart and no time for church or God in our busy schedules. Spiritually we were frozen in time.

Then, seven years after I had stopped going to church, something happened that jarred my heart. I got a wake-up call—literally. I was in Cincinnati, training for a technical support position in the appliance industry, and I stayed overnight at a hotel. At midnight I awoke to find myself wringing wet with sweat and the bed saturated from headboard to footboard. I sat straight up. Two angels were at the foot of my bed.

Their bodies were the purest, whitest white I had ever seen. It was almost as if they were translucent, and they seemed to be floating. I knew immediately that this was a supernatural event, but I didn't have a clue about what was actually going on. The huge angel on the left didn't move or say anything, but the angel on the right spoke to me. "One hundred fifty days," was all he said. Then both angels vanished, and the glowing white faded away.

I sat straight up. Two angels were at the foot of my bed.

I changed out of my soaked pajamas and moved over to the dry bed. Then I just lay there, stunned and confused, asking myself repeatedly, *What does 150 days mean?*

I spent the next couple of days trying to come up with a reasonable explanation for what had happened, but that just left me more confused. The only conclusion I could draw was that the world would end in 150 days and that God was somehow warning me. *But why me?* After three days of unrest, I finally decided that the experience had not been real and that I would never tell anyone about it. I simply denied the whole thing and moved on.

Several months later, a church on the outskirts of our community started to send a large bus around the area to pick up kids and take them to church. They asked if they could pick up our oldest son, Tyler. I remembered what an exciting adventure that had been for me, and we agreed. Our younger boy, Drew, was not old enough, so Sherry and I decided to take him to the local church while Tyler was gone.

There was a guest speaker that morning, and the service was so boring that all I wanted was for him to wrap it up so I could go home. Eager to get out, I glanced at my watch. It was 11:50 A.M. Just as I looked down, I began to experience a deep inner conviction and a stirring in my soul—not a feeling or a voice, but something much deeper. I couldn't relate the experience to anything the speaker was saying. It was almost as if God were carrying me into another world and drawing me to Him. This intense conviction went on for several minutes. When I again looked up, the preacher was inviting people to come to the altar and make a commitment to follow Jesus.

Suddenly unaware of anything or anyone around me, I walked to the front of the church and knelt. Then I heard myself say, "Jesus, I don't know who You are, but if You are who You say You are, I'll give You a chance to work in my life." I returned to my seat not realizing that I had just signed up for a personal relationship with Jesus.

As I drove home, I suddenly heard the voice of the angel who had spoken to me in my hotel room a few months earlier. It was obvious that I was the only one hearing it. *Do you remember the 150 days?* When I got home, I grabbed a calendar and counted the number of days it had been since the supernatural event I had decided hadn't really happened. Exactly 150 days! The 150 days hadn't meant the end of the world; it had meant the beginning of my new life with Jesus.

A deep commitment accompanied my decision, and I began to pursue God full force. I read the Bible and developed a life-changing relationship with Jesus. Within three years of the day I met God, my wife and sons committed their lives to Jesus as well, and soon I began feeling the desire to give up my career and go into a full-time ministry.

During that time, Jimmy, my sister, Debbie, and I attended my grandfather's funeral. There, Debbie recognized someone we had known as children, and she pointed him out to me. Amazed, I recognized the bus driver I had loved so much when I was small. I went straight up to him and told him that I remembered all the things he had done for me and what an impact he had made on my life. That kind elderly gentleman stood there and cried as I talked. So did I. A few months later, I heard that he had passed away.

In 1997, I made a leap of faith: I resigned from my secure job and began the ministry I had dreamed of. Today I serve full time in an inner-city bus ministry, but instead of bringing kids to church, I take church to kids—right in the streets of their urban neighborhoods. Every week I do the "dollar giveaway," and I give the same attention to our kids that my church bus driver gave to me. My models are my special friend, Roy, and that bus driver who set me on my spiritual journey so many years ago.

Joe is the founder of Urban Missions Ministries in North Carolina. He also spends quite a bit of time each year helping kids in Hollywood through the Oasis Ministry in Los Angeles. Joe and Sherry have been married eighteen years and take great joy in their sons, Tyler and Drew, who are now teenagers. You can reach him at urbanmissions@aol.com.

3

I WILL SURVIVE

Gloria Gaynor

Life contains two tragedies.
One is not to get your heart's desire;
the other is to get it.
GEORGE BERNARD SHAW

If anyone had asked me what my religion was before 1982, I would have said that I was a Christian. I believed that I had a strong faith in God—but honestly, I wouldn't have known Jesus if I had fallen over Him in the street. I had my own form of religion: I called on God when I had absolutely no other choice; otherwise, I was in control. I told myself that God was too busy to be bothered with my requests, but the truth was that, like most of us, I simply felt that I didn't need Him until I got desperate. Even then, I wanted Him on my terms.

I grew up in a poor home in Newark, New Jersey, with five brothers and one sister. Our little house was crowded, but after my father and mother separated, it felt empty, and so did I.

My emptiness followed me when I left home to start my singing career. In 1973, I got my first break when I recorded "Honey Bee," a song that opened the door to American disco and to a whole new world for me. My music brought me lots of attention, and money freed me from my difficult past. But they weren't enough to fill my emptiness.

I was afraid to be alone with my own thoughts. In my bachelorette apartment, I had the radio and TV going at the same time, all the time. When the TV programming ended, around 1:00 or 2:00 A.M., the national anthem would play, and then a preacher would come on. I never knew what the preacher said because I always made a mad dash from wherever I was in the apartment to shut off the TV before he spoke. Even in my emptiness, I just did not want to hear what God or any of His messengers had to say.

In 1975 my singing career really took off when I recorded "Never Can Say Goodbye," the first disco song ever to make it into the top forty on the pop music charts. Life was great! I won two Grammy Awards—number one album and number one song of the year. I was having great fun and filling my life with all the things I thought would make me happy. I deserved it. I worked hard and didn't want anything to stop me, and I especially didn't want God or any of His coworkers cramping my style.

My emptiness was always there, even in crowded auditoriums, concert halls, and amphitheaters.

But when I was home alone, I still had the radio and TV going at the same time, all the time. My emptiness was always there, even when I was singing to packed houses of screaming, loving fans in crowded auditoriums, concert halls, and amphitheaters. Nothing could fill it.

Just as I hit the pinnacle of my success, I began to realize that I had finally acquired all of the things that were supposed to make me happy. I had money, cars, furs, homes, jewelry, expensive clothes, a wonderful husband, fame, and access to anything I wanted. Yet I had a nagging sense that this wasn't all there was. I had done fun and wild things ad nauseam, but secretly I asked myself the six-million-dollar question: *Are we having fun yet?*

I was engaged in an inner battle. Although I didn't get completely sucked into it, I spent my waking hours in the professional music world of parties, drugs, sex, and rock 'n' roll—a way of life far removed from the way I had been raised. My childhood had been meager, but my upbringing had been moral and ethical, and my lifestyle as an adult was not satisfying. I often tried to pull away, but my desperate need for approval and love kept me emotionally tied to my peers. My head and my heart were playing tug-of-war.

Something had to give. One day I said a final good-bye to the party scene and my so-called friends and started on a quest to find the answer to one question: What makes a person who has everything feel fulfilled? In the depths of my soul, that question would not go away.

I started going to church because I felt that maybe my unrest was due to guilt for having ignored God when He had been so good to me. One Sunday morning in 1982, I sat in church absolutely bored to tears but determined to do my duty. So I bit my lip and stayed to the bitter end. Toward the close of the service, I had the wild thought that I should probably join the church. The problem was that on that very Sunday another family had the same idea. They were allowed to join—apparently on the condition that they believed that Jesus had lived and died for their sins and rose again. They had even been willing to tell others all about this.

Well, I didn't ask to join, because I didn't believe all that. I just couldn't say everything they wanted to hear. As a matter of fact, I knew Jesus only as a prophet, and I was afraid of putting a mere man on the same level as God. So I left.

When I got home, though, I kept asking myself, *Why do I need to know Him?* I couldn't shake off the question. Suddenly, I felt compelled to look in a Bible. I found one that someone had bought me as a gag gift. I blew off the dust, sat down at my dining-room table, and said, *Okay, God, I've got to have some answers. If You can talk to a priest, preacher, or rabbi, You can talk to me. I've been praying all my life, but I never needed Jesus or anyone else. Now, I'm really listening, and I need to know from You who this Jesus is.*

As I read, the answers just started flowing out. Everything was becoming clear, and I knew that this was where I could find out who Jesus was. I also knew the answer to my question: I would never find fulfillment in earthly things. Only God could give me the fulfillment I was seeking. That day, sitting alone in my dining room, reading that dusty, gag-gift Bible, I met God.

Suddenly, I felt compelled to look in a Bible. I found one that someone had bought me as a gag gift.

I was convinced that God was leading me to the answers to all my questions but that I needed to spend time alone with Him. So I walked away from my booming career, and for a full year we sat there together, God and I, at my dining-room table as He taught me about Jesus. We began in the Old Testament book of Isaiah. Then He led me through all the prophesies of the coming Messiah in the Old Testament and through Jesus' fulfillment of those prophesies in the New Testament.

During that year, God also taught me how to be alone without being lonely. I turned off the TV and the radio because I didn't need them anymore. I was never really alone because Jesus was always with me. I was getting validation from Him through the Bible, I was coming to understand His unconditional love, and He was answering all my questions. He was showing me that He was the only one who could fill my emptiness.

One year later, I reentered the music world. Singing with the greatest conviction, I recorded my hit song "I Will Survive." This time, I didn't feel any pull toward the party scene around me, I didn't need validation from my acquaintances in the business, and I wasn't tempted by the lure of fame and success. God and I were a team, and my work became for Him.

Over the past eighteen years I have matured emotionally and

spiritually and gained that deep feeling of affirmation and fulfillment I so badly needed—the kind that comes only from God. He
has shown me the gifts and attributes He has placed in me that
make me worthy of the respect of others. Most importantly, He
has shown me that all the things of the world cannot satisfy,
because only He can give me all that I need. Since the day I met
God, I have been truly blessed.

And guess what? I will survive!

Gloria has entered her fourth decade of success as a singer/
entertainer, having performed all over the world since the
early 1970s. Best known for her disco platinum hit "I Will
Survive," she was nominated for the Rock and Roll Music Hall of
Fame. Gloria has been married to Linwood Simon for twenty-one
years, and they reside happily in New Jersey.

MY CHOCOLATE SOLDIER

Maria Rogalski

Hope is the thing with feathers that perches in the soul.
EMILY DICKINSON

I would describe my childhood in two words: *disadvantaged beginnings.* I was born into a German family in communist Russia in 1933. I was just two years old when my father was taken prisoner and banished to Siberia. We never saw him again, and my mother was left alone to care for three children without help of any kind. She worked in a factory by day and washed clothes for wealthy people at night. Our living quarters were in a corner of a rag collector's humble home, and the four of us slept on the straw-covered floor. It was a meager existence.

I was eight years old when the German army advanced into Russia. When the war approached our village and shrapnel started flying over the roof of the house, my mother pleaded incessantly for help from the Germans. Eventually a German officer succumbed to her pleas and arranged for us to be taken back to Germany in a military transport.

But soon after, the war turned against the Germans, and we

began to flee from the advancing Russian army. Forever etched in my mind are the gruesome images of burning villages, men hanging on gallows at the side of the road, air raids at night, and bombs lighting up the night sky like a Christmas tree. Desolation was everywhere. Human kindness seemed not to exist. Many days I would think, *Why was I even born?*

As more and more of Germany fell to the control of the Allied Forces, refugees were packed into boxcars like human sardines. We had to stand back-to-back for hours. The trains wound their way to Schleswig Holstein, in the northernmost part of Germany. For a few years we made our home in one room of a large farmhouse in Arrild, which we were assigned to share with three other refugee families.

Oh, how I yearned for just one taste of that unattainable luxury!

When the war ended in May of 1945, it was very apparent that there was no future for us there. Even as we continued our constant fight for survival, my mom began to search for a way out for her and the three of us kids. There was little joy or hope in my life.

During those postwar days, we shared our single room with a pet chicken, which provided us with eggs to round out our meager diet of cornmeal porridge eaten hot for breakfast and sliced cold and fried for lunch and supper. In my deep hunger, I couldn't help but notice a British soldier who stopped daily right by the farmhouse where we lived. He always ate chocolate while he waited in his jeep for his officer to return from daily inspection rounds.

Oh, how I yearned for just one taste of that unattainable luxury! I told one of the refugee ladies about my overwhelming desire. She knew some English and helped me memorize a simple request. On my twelfth birthday, August 25, 1945, I gathered up all the courage I had, and with my pet chicken perched on my arm for moral support, I stepped up to the jeep and solemnly declared: "Today is my birthday. Please give me chocolate."

The tenderhearted soldier patiently helped me understand that he would return with some more chocolate at three o'clock that afternoon. Although nobody in the house believed that he would, he kept his promise and went out of his way to reappear at three o'clock to fulfill the birthday wish of a little "enemy" girl. That young man gave me hope for the first time in my life. Human compassion and kindness did exist, even amid the enmity of war. I never forgot that day.

Five years later, an opportunity came to start a new life in Canada. My cousin's aunt had immigrated there in the early 1900s and had sponsored cousin Olga, who joined her in 1949. The following year, Olga's brother-in-law sponsored us. So we immigrated to Canada, where I celebrated my seventeenth birthday.

By the time I was nineteen, even in this new land of promise, I had been feeling a deep emptiness inside for some time. The trauma of my past and the transition to the free world was difficult for me, and I began to look for something that would give me peace and purpose. Why was I here, and why had I survived when so many others hadn't? I was invited to attend services at an evangelical church, where I soon learned that the peace of heart I was searching for can be found only through a personal encounter with the living, true God. Oh, how I longed to have that encounter!

I had grown up without any kind of spiritual influence. I didn't even know if God existed. In communist Russia we were forbidden even to talk about God. When I first heard that there was a God who actually cared about me personally, I was truly excited. For two years, I waited for something spectacular to occur—something accompanied by thunder or lightning or perhaps majestic out-of-this-world music—when I would dramatically meet God. But nothing like that happened.

Then one day as I listened to our pastor talk about the Parable of the Prodigal Son, I was deeply touched. The pastor explained that although the father in the parable loved his son and wanted him to return to enjoy all the privileges and blessings of the father's house, he did not go after his son and drag him home by the scruff of his neck. No! The turning point came when the wayward son came to his senses and said, "'I will set out and go to my father and say to him: Father, I have sinned against heaven and against you'" (Luke 15:18). The pastor further explained that it is the same with God, our heavenly Father. He loves us and longs for us to "come home" where we belong, but the choice of coming is a personal decision that we all must make for ourselves.

At that moment, God opened my eyes and, like the prodigal, I recognized my lost condition. I asked Jesus to come into my life and forgive my sins. That was the day I committed my life to Him. There was no thunder and lightning and no heavenly music—just tears of repentance and joy. My search had ended. I had met God and finally discovered meaning in my life and my purpose for being here. I was never the same again.

As the years went by, I never forgot that British soldier who had given me chocolate on my twelfth birthday. That simple act of kindness had given me a glimmer of hope that there was something or someone good in this world. Almost forty years after that day, I began a serious search for my "chocolate soldier," who had so touched me during the horrific aftermath of war.

I began a serious search for my "chocolate soldier."

I set out to find him, and through a series of newspaper articles, including a letter to Queen Elizabeth of England, the incredible happened.

In September of 1993, after a ten-year search, I found Cornelius O'Sullivan, of Cardiff, South Wales, who had served with the Royal Welch Fusiliers. Thanks to the British Broadcasting Corporation, which flew me to England for Armistice Day that year, I met this special soldier and thanked him personally—in proper English this time—for his act of kindness in the terrible aftermath of an awful war so many years earlier.

Reflecting back, I can see that God was there with me all the time—especially through my chocolate soldier—letting me know that He cared about the small details of my life. Jesus had been setting the stage all along, arranging circumstances so I could meet Him one day in that church in Canada and finally find the meaning of my life. My search had ended, and an exciting new journey had begun in the shelter of His love.

A freelance writer living in Winnipeg, Canada, Maria has published articles in various Christian magazines and daily newspapers. An inspirational speaker, she is president of the Manitoba Christian Writers' Association. She has shared her story about her chocolate soldier in many schools and churches, including Calvary Church in Santa Ana, California. Married to Hans for almost forty-six years, she has four grown children and ten grandchildren.

5

THE ALMIGHTY AND THE GUN

Eddie Charles Spencer

Who overcomes by force hath overcome but half his foe.
JOHN MILTON

I grew up among the poorest of the poor in a small cotton-growing town in the Mississippi delta. My family lived in a raggle-taggle, three-room shotgun shack on the back side of town. The older kids slept together in the middle room, while the baby slept up front in the bed with Momma and Daddy. There was never enough food to go around, and mostly we wore hand-me-downs. We were so bad off that my family not only got clothes donated from white people, but we also got things passed on from other blacks just as poor as we were.

When I was six years old, I didn't have shoes to wear to school, so Momma sent me off in a pair of my sister's. When I stepped into my first-grade classroom, all the kids looked down at my feet and started to laugh. "Look at Eddie Spencer! He's got little-girl shoes on!" I felt hurt and ashamed, but mostly I felt angry—angry at the kids for making fun of me, angry at my parents for not being able to provide me with even basic necessities, and angry at the world for giving me my lot in life. Right then and there, I decided to retaliate against all those who had hurt me.

A few months later, I found my daddy's hidden pistol and accidentally shot myself in the hand. As I watched the reaction of people around me, I realized that I had stumbled upon a source of power—"the almighty gun"—a power to control, wound, and kill. If I had found that weapon as a young child today, I might have brought it to school, loaded and cocked, ready to get my revenge. But times were less complicated in 1968, and I just took revenge on folks with my fists and my tongue. It would be a few years down the road before I was ready to take advantage of the power of a gun.

I realized I had stumbled upon a source of power—"the almighty gun"—a power to control, wound, and kill.

The following year, I noticed some older boys hanging out in my neighborhood who seemed to have everything I wanted. I started running with them, and we formed a little gang. As the youngest, I desperately wanted the older boys to accept me, so I did whatever they told me to do. At first we did small things together like taking lunch money from kids at school and snatching toys out of people's yards. Over time, we began to steal from stores and homes.

Before I was eight, the older boys also showed me how to sniff gasoline. It didn't take long for me to become a "gasoholic," and I stayed hooked on gas for years. Drugs were not as common as they are today, so my friends and I got high on what was readily available. Eventually I started smoking marijuana and popping pills. Drugs gave me the courage I needed to continue my criminal activities, and they seemed to suppress my emptiness and guilt.

Right after my tenth birthday, I found myself standing before a judge in juvenile court. Thinking it would turn me around, he sent me to training school. Only he was wrong. I was so hooked on crime and drugs that over the next five years I went in and out of training school four more times. Every time I got back on the streets, I thought I was slicker than the time before. I was addicted to violence, and nothing could stop me.

By then I had quit running with the gang. I had never forgotten the sense of power behind the barrel of a gun, and I had begun to take that power into my own hands. Working on my own, I robbed people at gunpoint in the streets as well as in their houses. I particularly liked sticking a pistol into people's faces while I made my demands. I carried a gun everywhere I went and found myself living for only two things: a reputation and a dollar bill. I would do anything and everything to get those for myself. As a result, people feared me, and that was exactly how I liked it.

The deeper I got into the street life, the colder and harder I became. When I was thirteen, I watched a guy walk out in the street and unload a .44 caliber pistol into another guy's chest. I found myself laughing because I didn't care about anyone's life but my own.

Not too long after that, I even tried to shoot my own father. I would have killed him, I guess, except that when I fired, I missed. Before I turned sixteen, I'd been shot three times myself. I took one bullet during a street fight and two more while committing robberies. But even bullets didn't stop me. My crimes kept on increasing. I was totally out of control.

I grew more and more devoid of feelings, until I had just enough left to know that I needed to stop feeling anything. So, I filled myself with more drugs and violence to stop the pain. But I just became more and more miserable. Instead of feeling nothing, I felt nothing but fear and pain. Still, I couldn't let anyone know what I felt. My reputation wouldn't let me. I needed relief, but I couldn't find it anywhere in the streets, and I couldn't quit my lifestyle either. It was all I knew.

Finally, in the fall of 1979, I got caught up in a month-long robbing spree. One night I broke into a house, jammed my pistol into the face of a sleeping man, and demanded his money. He looked me right in the eye and said some words I sure didn't want to hear. They burned in my ears as I took his money and headed back to the streets, and although I tried to ignore them, I could never shake them from my memory.

My violence continued in fast forward until, only a few months later, I found myself standing before a judge. This time I was being tried as an adult, not as a juvenile, and I faced the possibility of the death penalty for the crimes I'd committed. I had robbed a man in his own home and, for no reason at all, beaten him into a coma. Then I'd stabbed a fellow inmate in the city jail. Amazingly, neither man died, so instead of getting the death penalty, I was sentenced to ten years mandatory at Parchman Penitentiary for armed robbery and attempted murder.

I jammed my pistol into the face of a sleeping man and demanded his money. He looked me right in the eye and said some words I sure didn't want to hear.

There I was, only seventeen years old and already headed for a stay in Mississippi's infamous penitentiary. For the first time ever—if only for a brief moment—I felt the complete futility of my life. Afraid of facing reality, I quickly shook off the feeling. I entered Parchman on June 26, 1980, sold out to the same desire I had had in the streets—to be tough enough to earn myself a reputation.

Inside prison I started boxing. I had found myself a new weapon, and I quickly built myself the name I was after. I became so good with my hands that I lost only two matches the whole time I fought. Soon, I had even the roughest guys looking up to me, and that thrilled me. At the same time, though, I began to suspect that everything I'd worked so hard to get would eventually fail me. I was just too scared to admit it, even to myself.

Then one day in June of 1982, I was sitting alone on my prison cot thinking about how I could increase my reputation even more. I felt I had to outdo everything I'd done up until then. I began making plans to use my "shank," a handmade knife I kept hidden in my locker, to kill two guys I didn't like. As I sat there contemplating murder, I thought I heard God speaking to me. I'm not sure how I knew it was His voice. I just did.

Eddie, the voice said, *it's either your way or My way. You can continue with what you're planning, or you can let it go and give your life to the Lord Jesus Christ. You've got to choose.*

As I sat there listening to this message from God, the words that man had spoken to me years before as I held a pistol in his face suddenly echoed in my mind: *You can have the money, but what you really need is to give your life to the Lord Jesus Christ!*

At that very moment, I heard those words in a new way, and for the first time ever I saw things clearly. All my life I had tried to find meaning and fulfillment through drugs, violence, and a reputation, but I had failed. Now God was offering me another way— His way. I couldn't resist. Sitting right there with my hand still touching the knife I had planned to use to commit murder, I found myself giving my life to Jesus Christ—just like the person on the other side of my gun all those years before had told me I should do.

Beginning right then, God began to transform me into a man I never imagined I could be. A young white catfish farmer named Lee Holland was leading a Bible study at the prison, and I started going. Up until then, I had only been able to read as well as a third grader. Once Lee Holland got hold of me, I developed such a hunger for God's Word that I learned to read every last sentence in it. Some days I'd study my Bible for hours and hours.

God also began enabling me to control my anger. Although it was very difficult for me to do, I gave up boxing and the now meaningless reputation I had worked so hard to earn. Once I did,

God gave me the opportunity to begin traveling throughout Mississippi to tell my story to young people in schools, churches, and local organizations. Over the next few years, I gave my message of hope to more than 130,000 students.

As I studied the Bible, I learned that once I let God take control of my life, I would become a new creature—my old self would pass away and I would become new. And I did, but it took time. In fact, I spent almost six and a half more years in the prison system before I got to the place where I was ready to leave. But when I was finally granted clemency and walked out of jail on January 14, 1988, I no longer even resembled the man I'd been when I entered Parchman. Not only was I a free man; I was also a totally changed man.

I soon discovered that, for me, living for Jesus was much easier inside prison than outside. In Parchman there had been restrictions and rules to control my actions as well as the safety and security of a familiar system. The day I left prison, I'd never held a job, earned a full week's paycheck, or paid rent. I'd never even had a driver's license. I was twenty-five years old and lacked all of life's basic skills.

I had a lot to learn about living on the outside, and I had a lot of needs, but I received everything I needed at just the right time. God's immediate provision was a place to live. Jim and Michelle Young, a young white couple from Jackson, took me into their home for the first few months I was out of prison. They were just the first of many people—both white and black—who came into my life to encourage me, teach me, and give me hope as I adjusted to living in a society I knew very little about. I am deeply thankful for every one of them.

But I am especially grateful to the man, whose name I now know is George Walsh, who had the courage to tell me the truth even when I had a gun in his face. My life really began the day I met George and he told me about God.

After leaving prison, Eddie worked in Jackson, Mississippi, as Urban Area Director of Young Life, a ministry to teenagers. In 1989, *USA Today* honored him as one of fifty national drug-fighting heroes, and in 1990 he served on the Presidential Drug Task Force. In 1995, Eddie returned to his hometown of Hollandale, Mississippi, where he now lives with the very people who knew him as a kid-criminal. He operates his own restaurant and catering business and is currently working on a memoir of his life. He and his wife, Betty, consider themselves richly blessed by her son, Lincoln, and his daughter, Sharon.

6

BEYOND THE STARS: AN ASTRONOMER'S QUEST

Dr. Hugh Ross

Science without religion is lame; religion without science is blind.
ALBERT EINSTEIN

I was born in Montreal and raised in Vancouver, Canada. My parents were morally upright but not religious—a description that also fit our neighbors. While I was growing up, I did not know any Christians or serious followers of any other religion.

Though my neighborhood was poor, its public schools were outstanding and its libraries well equipped. By age seven, I was reading physics books as fast as I could check them out; by eight, I had decided to make astronomy my career. Over the next several years, my study of the "big bang" convinced me that the universe had a beginning and, thus, a Beginner. But like the astronomers whose books I read, I imagined that the Beginner must be distant and noncommunicative.

My high school history studies disturbed me, though, for they showed that the peoples of the world take their religions very seriously. When I learned that the European philosophers of the Enlightenment largely discounted religion, my initial response was to study their works. What I discovered, however, were inconsistencies, contradictions, evasions, and circular reasoning.

The obvious next step was to turn to the books that the world's major religions hold sacred. If God the Creator had spoken through any of them (and I thought that He probably had not), His authorship would be obvious because the communication would be true. I reasoned that if men invent their own religion, their teachings will reflect human error but that if the Creator communicates, His message will be error free and as internally consistent as the facts of nature. So I used the facts of history and science to test each of the holy books.

Initially my task was easy. After only a few hours (in some cases less) of reading some of the books, I found one or more statements that were clearly at odds with the facts of history and science. I also noted a writing style best described as esoteric and mysterious, which seemed inconsistent with the character of the Creator as implied by the facts of nature.

Then I pulled out the Bible that the Gideons had given me several years earlier as part of their distribution program in the public schools. I found the text of the Bible noticeably different. It was simple, direct, and specific. I was amazed at the amount of incredibly detailed historical and scientific (that is, testable) material in it. The first page of the Bible especially caught my attention. Not only did it correctly describe the major events in the creation of life on earth, but it also placed those events in the scientifically correct order and properly identified earth's initial conditions. Given the scientific information available to the ancients, the author could not possibly have known this information without some sort of divine help.

For the next year and a half, I spent about an hour a day searching the Bible for scientific and historical inaccuracies. Finally, I had to admit that I could find none and that this book could only have come from the Creator Himself. I recognized that the

Bible was unique in describing God and His dealings with man from a perspective outside of the dimensions that we humans experience (length, width, height, and time). Further, the accuracy of its prophecies (with regard to the rise and fall of empires, the future of Arab-Israeli conflicts, and so on) and of its references to science (the characteristics of the cosmos, Earth, biological systems, etc.) convinced me that the Bible was as reliable as the laws of physics. My only rational option was to trust the Bible's authority to the same degree that I trusted the laws of physics.

By this time, I clearly understood that Jesus Christ was the creator of the universe, that He had paid the price only a morally perfect person could pay for my imperfect response both to God and to fellow humans, and that eternal life with Him would be mine if I would receive His pardon and give Him His rightful place of authority over my life. As I continued my studies, planning to make astrophysics my vocation, my new discoveries about God as the creator of the laws of physics became richer and more meaningful.

However, I also understood enough Scripture to know that this commitment could not be a secret one. It had to be public, and that meant letting my peers, professors, and family know about it. I feared the contempt and ridicule that surely would come. So for several months I hesitated.

During those months I experienced a strange sense of confusion. For the first time in my life, my grades dropped, and I had difficulty solving problems. I was discovering the meaning of the passage in the Bible that says that when a man rejects what he knows and understands to be true about God, his thinking becomes futile and his mind darkened (Romans 1:21). The consequences spelled out in the succeeding verses chilled me.

I knew what I had to do, but my pride seemed too great. One evening I prayed, asking God to take away my resistance and make me a Christian. I prayed this way for six hours, with no apparent answer. Finally, I realized that Jesus Christ would not force Himself upon anyone, even if asked. It was up to me to humble myself and invite Him in.

And this is what I did. At 1:06 in the morning, I signed my name to the "decision statement" at the back of my Gideon Bible, acknowledging that I had asked Jesus Christ to be my Lord and Savior.

Right away, I felt assured that God would never let me go— that I was His forever. My fear of being

I prayed this way for six hours, with no apparent answer.

ridiculed by unbelievers subsided day by day as I learned how to share my discoveries of spiritual truth with fellow students and faculty. Nevertheless, without the benefits of fellowship with other Christians, I found that my growth in Christlikeness was stunted.

Every once in a while I would visit a church, only to find a cult or people who called themselves Christians but did not take the Bible seriously. At last, upon arriving at Cal Tech for postdoctoral studies, I met a serious Christian, Dave Rogstad. Dave invited me to attend a seminar on applying biblical principles to daily living. There I sat with 16,000 committed Christians, all in one building. I was overwhelmed to find that so many Christians existed, and I was helped and humbled by the things I learned.

Within weeks of that seminar, I found myself not only attending home Bible studies, but also helping lead them. Dave challenged me to begin sharing my faith with nonscientists. I was surprised to observe that unlike scientists, who tend to struggle more with their wills in coming to Christ, the nonscientists I met tended to struggle more with their minds. Once they saw convincing evidence that God exists, that Jesus is God, and that the Bible is true, they readily gave their lives to Christ. What a joy!

I began spending more and more time telling others about the evidence I had discovered. Within a year, I was serving full time as a lay minister for Sierra Madre Congregational Church. Ten years later, in 1985, when breakthrough discoveries in the sciences virtually sealed the scientific case for the God of the Bible, a group of friends urged me to form an organization, Reasons To Believe, to communicate this new evidence as widely as possible.

As an astronomer, I have achieved my ultimate quest.

Ever since I stopped resisting God and entrusted my life to Him, my joy in knowing Him and in sharing His truth with both scientists and nonscientists has grown greater every day. Both my studies and my heart tell me that He is the Truth, and there is nothing in this world for which I would trade my relationship with Him. As an astronomer, I have achieved my ultimate quest: My education led me to the stars; my faith led me beyond.

D r. Ross earned a B.S. in physics from the University of British Columbia and an M.S. and Ph.D. in astronomy from the University of Toronto. He then conducted research on quasars and galaxies as a postdoctoral fellow at the California Institute of Technology. Today he directs Reasons To Believe, an institute founded to research and proclaim the factual basis for faith in God and the Bible. Hugh lives in Southern California with his wife, Kathy, and sons, Joel and David. Visit RTB at www.reasons.org.

7

PEOPLE LIKE US DON'T GO TO PRISON!

Bonnie Lang

Success has ruined many a man.
BENJAMIN FRANKLIN

There we were, standing at the altar about to be married. Jim was my knight in shining armor—young, handsome, and ambitious. A top graduate of the Air Force Academy, he was everything I had always wanted. I just knew he would meet all of my needs—he'd love me, provide for me, and take care of my self-worth for me. I would be a totally fulfilled woman.

Of course, his thoughts went along the same lines. His young bride would take care of all of his needs. He wouldn't have to cook any more meals or worry about the laundry; he would always be admired and adored; and his sex drive would always be satisfied.

What great expectations we had!

Our zeal to succeed energized the first few years of our marriage. A highly respected pilot, Jim quickly rose in rank. I pursued my career as a teacher and within two years received our state's "Outstanding Young Woman of the Year" award for my work in the classroom and the community. But although we worked hard, we didn't feel fulfilled. So Jim left the Air Force to go into business for himself, and we moved to California to pursue our dreams.

We made a list of our life goals. At the top was Jim's determination to make a million dollars before he was forty. Then came more travel, vacation homes, social status, sports cars, airplanes, children, more money—and more! We spent the next few years pursuing these dreams, and by the time he was thirty-two, Jim had accomplished all of his ambitions. But we still felt empty. All that the world had promised would make us happy had left both of us unfulfilled. Money, prestige, titles, honors, homes, planes, cars, and cruises brought us only temporary pleasure.

Jim's ambition pushed him further and further away from his family as he pursued the elusive American Dream. His type-A personality and drive for stature in the business world drove a deep wedge into our relationship. The demands of four children under six years of age occupied all of my time and energy, but our four young girls hardly knew their father because he left before dawn and came home long past their bedtimes. I spent many lonely nights at home, and I ended up disillusioned and resentful.

Jim was also experiencing severe feelings of emptiness, often wondering, *Where do we go from here?* But neither of us knew where to turn. In desperation we tried transcendental meditation, holistic medicine, and the power of the mind. Still we found no solace. Nothing seemed to fill the void we both felt.

At the height of our success we were invited to a dinner at the Fairmont Hotel in San Francisco. We really did not want to attend because the speaker had been involved in Watergate-related crimes, and we weren't interested in hearing a convicted criminal rehash that scandal. After refusing the invitation several times, we reluctantly accepted.

We were both taken aback when the speaker, Chuck Colson, referred to Watergate only to say that it had brought him into a life-changing relationship with God. Although Jim and I had both attended church on and off since childhood, we had never heard anything like what Colson had to say. He talked about how God had changed his heart and given him a new direction in life and how that had carried him through his ordeal and sustained him while he was in prison. Stunned by what we had heard, we were silent as we left the room that night.

A few days after the dinner, our host for the evening gave us a copy of *Born Again*, Colson's book about his conversion experience. In it, he explained how in his despair he had called out to Jesus Christ and asked Him to come into his life and deliver him from the misery he was experiencing. Although our circumstances were hardly the same—I had never even known anyone who had been in prison—I somehow felt that I knew the despair and longing he described.

> *Stunned by what we had heard, we were silent as we left the room that night.*

I needed something, but I had been unable to find it. I wasn't even sure that God existed. I thought that God was a nice idea for those who needed Him, but I had never thought that I was someone who did. I had lived my life based on the notion that I could control my own destiny and find happiness through worldly success. Clearly, it wasn't working.

When I finished reading Colson's incredible story, I sat alone in my bedroom and, at the age of thirty-three, found myself saying to God, *If You really exist, please come into my life and take over. I can't do it on my own any longer. I just don't know how to be fulfilled or happy. If You're real, please reveal Yourself to me.*

There were no clanging gongs or clashing symbols—just a quiet submission of my will to His. God knew that I was not one for big emotional displays. I was a practical, down-to-earth woman. I had made the commitment, and I was ready for whatever came next. So I waited.

A few months later, Jim and I were invited to an executive

seminar at the headquarters of Campus Crusade for Christ in Arrowhead Springs, California. We weren't sure what the seminar was about, but we were attracted by the impressive list of successful men lined up as keynote speakers.

The first evening, Dr. Bill Bright, founder and president of Campus Crusade, greeted us and explained briefly that the one thing all the speakers had in common was their relationship with Jesus Christ. He said that we too could have this relationship with our Creator by confessing our sins and asking Christ to come into our lives.

After the session, we were asked to go off to a quiet place by ourselves, write out a list of all our sins, ask God to forgive us, and then destroy the list. This was symbolic of what Christ had done when He died for us on the cross. He removed all of our sins and took the punishment upon Himself by dying for them. When Jim returned to the room that night, I knew something dramatic was happening to him. The next morning Dr. Bright invited us to his office, and there Jim prayed to receive Christ into his life.

Whereas my prayer a few months back had been a quiet surrender, Jim's was a stirring and exciting moment. He felt as though the weight of the world had been lifted from his shoulders and that he was finally free. He was ready to "conquer hell with a water pistol." If fireworks and rockets go off in anyone's soul, they did in his. I was delighted to have this common bond with him.

He was ready to "conquer hell with a water pistol."

That weekend the Bible became so real to us that we couldn't get enough of it. We were so hungry to learn about God and what He wanted in our lives that we went to nearly every Christian camp, conference, and event we could find. God began to teach us how He intended for us to live.

Our twelve-year marriage was refashioned after God's pattern of selflessness, sacrifice, respect, and unconditional love for each other and for God. Once filled with bitterness and resentment, our relationship now was full of joy. Money was no longer a god, people were more important than projects, and our goals centered on what we could do for God. God trained us and changed our hearts in an incredibly short time.

God knew that our faith was about to be tested.

About two years into our new life, everything came crashing down when the federal government indicted Jim on fifteen counts of mail fraud connected with the firm he had established nine years earlier. While remaining president of that company, Jim had started another one and put all his energy into the new venture, thus not "minding the store." He had ignored things that he should have dealt with, kept quiet when he should have spoken up, and left important decisions to the lawyers and advisors he had hired for the company. Well, his name *was* at the top, so the buck stopped there. He was responsible for all the company's actions, and now he was being punished for wrong choices he had made years before he knew God.

But did Jim deserve to be indicted? Why would God let that happen? Why now? Hadn't He cleansed and purified us? Weren't we now living the kind of life that was pleasing to Him? We struggled with these questions for months.

After two years of lawyers and hearings and a six-week trial, Jim was convicted on eight counts and sentenced to five years in prison. *Prison!* People like us don't go to prison! How could this be happening to us?

By the time Jim was to begin serving his sentence, the judge had reduced his time to one year in prison with four years of probation. This was great news, because people sentenced to one year are, without incident, usually in prison for only about four months. But would Jesus be enough to take us through the times ahead? Jim's business had suffered under the strain of the trial, and we had to use most of our money to pay for his defense. We had little left but the roof over our heads and the hope that God would see us through.

As I clung to the promise in Philippians 4:19—"My God will meet all your needs according to his glorious riches in Christ Jesus"—God proved to me that He was indeed sufficient to meet my every need. He comforted me with His peace and sheltered me under His wings. Never once did I spend a sleepless night jumping at the creaking of the floors or the howling of the wind about the house. He protected my children from humiliation and surrounded us with friends who loved us and helped us meet our financial needs. He gave me the strength I needed to run the household, lead a large weekly Bible study, and drive ten hours to and from the prison to visit Jim. He drew us closer as a family and helped restore the girls' relationship with their father as they spent uninterrupted hours just visiting, playing games, or walking and talking together at the prison.

When Jim returned home, there was nothing left of his business. A friend offered him a position with a company in Norman, Oklahoma, and after six months of commuting by plane each week, Jim packed up our family and headed to Oklahoma to begin again. We found a wonderful new church, Jim began to regain financial stability, and we started to rebuild our broken lives.

Then, one year later, our world was shattered again.

Our faith was once again severely tested when the IRS ran a sting operation on the company because they suspected one of its officers of criminal activity. My worst fears were realized when we found ourselves back in court facing charges of violation of probation just by being involved with this company.

Jim was as devastated as I was. Why hadn't God forewarned us not to take this job? This was Jim's chance to start over and prove that he could do things on the up and up. He was doing everything right this time—he was paying attention and minding the store. How could he have ended up at a company that was already under investigation for wrongdoing?

The judge showed no mercy. He found Jim guilty of violating his probation and sentenced him to return to prison to serve the rest of his term. My heart broke as Jim was shackled and led from the courtroom. He was taken to a prison camp about a one-hour drive from our home. By then our children were teenagers, and the force of the trauma shattered them.

It had been twenty years since I'd been in the workforce, and I had no prospects of a job. For the first time in my life, I was emotionally drained to the point of depression. Nothing I did could pull me out of the despair I was experiencing. I continued to go to church, pray, and study the Bible, but the song had gone from my heart. I could not understand why God had allowed Jim to be sent back to prison.

By then our children were teenagers, and the force of the trauma shattered them.

One evening, I wandered into a Bible study that was just beginning in our church. It was on the book of James, and quite unexpectedly, God lifted the veil that was clouding my vision. Since becoming Christians, Jim and I had learned to thank God in all circumstances, and we had paid lip service to James 1:2, which says to "consider it pure joy...whenever you face trials of many kinds." But somehow I had missed the next two verses. As I read them that night, a light suddenly came on: "because you know that the testing of your faith develops perserverance. Perserverance must finish its work so that you may be mature and complete, not lacking anything." Those verses lifted me out of my despair and set me free.

Now I knew why God had put me in these circumstances. He was giving me my heart's desire to be "mature and complete, not lacking anything." That's what God had in mind for me, for Jim, and for our children. How could anyone dispute that? He did have a purpose in mind for all of this pain, and I was to be the benefactor.

From that time on, I had peace despite our circumstances. I watched daily as God once again proved Himself to us in miraculous ways. He provided jobs, scholarships, grants, and gifts to care for us financially. And just as He provided faithfully for us on the "outside," He also began a mighty work in Jim's life on the "inside."

He helped Jim realize his need to surrender totally to Christ and showed him that He had a plan for him in every circumstance of life. God used Jim to help begin a full-scale revival in which prisoners found new life and hope in Jesus. He used our Oklahoma church family in a wonderful way as well. They donated thousands of books for a Christian library in the prison chapel, brought laughter and joy when they came to play softball with the inmates, sang and preached in the chapel services, led Bible studies, sent cards and letters, befriended the friendless, and brought hope to the hopeless.

In July 1989, ten years after the initial indictment, Jim came home. God granted many of our hearts' desires during that time, and He has granted many more since. He made it possible for Jim to have a job immediately upon his release and eventually to become the executive director of the Bill Glass Prison Ministry in Dallas, Texas.

Our lives have not been what we anticipated when we stood at the altar in 1965, naively thinking that another person or the riches of this world could meet our deepest needs. Little did we know, way back at the Fairmont Hotel when we heard former inmate Chuck Colson tell his story, that our paths would be so similar. God led us to that meeting to draw us into a personal relationship with Him and to give us the encouragement we would need to get through the devastating journey that lay ahead.

Neither Jim nor I would trade the experiences we've had for anything, because God has taught us that the trials of life make us strong. We have been from riches to rags to God's riches...and we are blessed.

Bonnie is the mother of four daughters and the grandmother of seven. One of her daughters, Terry Jones, sings with the Christian quartet "Point of Grace." Bonnie works full time for the Bill Glass Ministries in Dallas, Texas, which brings the message of salvation into the prisons of the world. You can reach her at bonnie@glassweb.com.

8

SAVING PRIVATE WERTHEIM

Fred Wertheim

I don't think of all the misery, but of the beauty that still remains.
ANNE FRANK

I was born June 23, 1925, in Waldorf Thuringen, Germany, the son of a Jewish immigrant baker who was a hero in my eyes. I lived with my parents, my dear old grandmother, and my two older sisters. We were all very close, in part because we had to stick together. Our town had very few Jews among its two thousand people—ten families, to be exact. As a young boy, I had to look among the non-Jews for playmates because the only other Jewish children were my sisters and an older girl down the street. It didn't bother me to have gentile friends, but I noticed that it started bothering them to have a Jewish one.

By the time I was eight, most Germans were well on their way to accepting the Aryan philosophy of Hitler. I knew that it had permeated my neighborhood when my best friends suddenly did not want to play with me anymore. My parents were convinced that Hitler would soon lose his popularity and that things would get better once again for the Jews. Instead they got worse. I was being beaten up in school just because I was Jewish. One day during an awful beating, I looked up and saw my teacher standing at the schoolroom window, just watching the beating and not making the slightest effort to help me.

Our family finally decided to leave Germany and start over in America. However, wanting to leave and getting out of the country were two different things. Because of immigration quotas, we had to apply to the consulate for clearance. We were given a number—48,878—the number of people who would be allowed to leave Germany before us. It seemed almost impossible that we would ever get to go.

Meanwhile, life got more difficult by the day. On July 2, 1938, I became bar mitzvah. I was the last Jewish boy to participate in the ceremony in our district. German Jewish children were now being kicked out of the public schools and families were being harassed. And that was only the beginning of the end.

Only four months later came Kristallnacht, the most horrifying night of my life.

Only four months later came Kristallnacht, the most horrifying night of my life. They lined up our family in our front yard. My father was violently beaten and got his teeth knocked out, and then he was taken away to a camp. All I could do was watch. My synagogue, along with hundreds of others, was destroyed.

Six days later, Jewish children were expelled from all the schools. At the same time, every Jewish male thirteen or older was conscripted for "labor camps." Fortunately, I was overlooked because I was small for my age.

Before long, entire Jewish families were being deported to the death camps. For some mysterious reason, my family was spared, although all of our valuables were taken and every form of communication was ripped out of our home. My mother and sisters and I lived in seclusion in our ransacked home. We had our bags packed, and we were just waiting for the next blow.

Suddenly one day, out of the blue, my father was sent back home. Then, to our amazement, our immigration number came up. In May of 1941, our family left what had become Hitler's Germany for what we saw to be heaven on earth—America.

We struggled to adjust to our new life; at least, being sixteen, I learned the English language quickly. Ironically, after having been in the States only two years, I was drafted into the U.S. Army. I was proud to get the chance to defend this country that had given me freedom. I was also still so angry at Germany that I couldn't wait to go back there to get revenge.

After training in America and Britain, I was assigned to a front-line unit in the invasion of Europe on D Day, arriving within an hour of the first wave of soldiers to hit the beach. Six hundred of our men died immediately. But again I survived. With some of my platoon, I fought my way through France and across the Rhine River into my native Germany—only to be captured by the Germans!

The Germans talked among themselves loudly enough for us to hear. I was the only one who understood what they were saying, and my body started to shake. Some of my buddies asked me, "What's happening? How come you're ready to pass out?" I told them, "This is the way it's going to be: They don't know what to do with us, and so they're going to shoot us." Miraculously, a few moments later they changed their minds. Instead of shooting us, they led us to a truck to take us to a prisoner-of-war camp.

At one point on the long journey, we were in a German half-track going down a treacherous road when the driver fell asleep. It slid off the road and flipped upside down on top of us. Two Germans lay dead next to me. The half-track was so heavy with equipment that I couldn't move, and my face was lodged down in the mud. Then some water started to come up around me, and I lay there trapped, sure that I was going to drown.

Believing that my life was over, I said the Sh'ma and then called out to God, pleading for His help. It was the first time I had cried out to God, and I knew He must have heard because at that moment quite a few of my German captors lifted the half-track and slid me out from under it. My enemy had spared my life.

Two Germans lay dead next to me.

At last we arrived at Stalag 11B, a camp near Hanover. The men there were just skin and bones, too weak to work. Many couldn't even stand up. Our heads were shaved, and clothes were burned regularly due to lice infestation. Our breakfast and lunch were combined into one "meal" of a tin can filled with black coffee. In the late afternoon we were given a stew that contained vegetables and occasionally a few strings of horsemeat. It smelled so rotten that I literally held my nose while I was eating. Once in a while, very late at night, some Germans from outside the camp would throw food over the fence and run away. It reminded me that not all Germans were Hitlerites.

In April 1945, the Allied Forces conquered Germany, and General Montgomery's Ninth Division liberated Stalag 11B. After I recovered from the effects of my imprisonment, I was sent home. I was going home just before Mother's Day. What a gift! I felt so grateful to be back in a safe place. However, my emotions were battling.

God had done so many good things for me. He had brought my immediate family out of Germany. He had kept me alive in a prisoner-of-war camp. First I had escaped from Hitler as a Jewish refugee; then I was liberated as an American prisoner of war. Yet I still didn't feel free, and I didn't know why God had saved me and not others. I believed in God and felt that He had saved me for a purpose, but I didn't know what my purpose was. All I knew to do was to thank Him for the miracles. That helped. I decided that I should just go on living and hope that someday God would show me so that I could feel free.

Not long after my return, I married Laura, a nice Jewish girl from my synagogue, and we settled down in the Bronx. I worked as a mail carrier, and Laura and I raised two sons. Life went smoothly until the day I got a phone call from my oldest son, Steve, who had moved to California after graduating from college. As he spoke to me, I could not believe my ears, even though his words were clear: "Dad, Mom…I've come to believe in Jesus as Messiah."

I did not take the news well at all. After all I had been through, I heard my own flesh and blood turn against me. We spent an hour and a half on the phone with Steve. Laura yelled and screamed, and I sat in stunned silence, just listening and crying, overcome with depression. For weeks after Steve's phone call, I would just suddenly break down in tears on my mail route. People asked me what was wrong, but I couldn't tell them. I was ashamed to let them know that my son had betrayed me and become a Christian.

> *"I want to meet the man who did this to you, and I want to kill him."*

Steve tried to explain that his decision to believe in Jesus was not intended to hurt me. It was a decision based on conviction—the conviction that Jesus was the Messiah of Israel. Steve told me about a Mr. Goldstein who had originally told him about Jesus. Mr. Goldstein was a Jew for Jesus, and Steve had joined his Bible study meeting. That's where my son became convinced of his spiritual need and of Jesus' sufficiency.

While I was depressed over Steve's decision, I became very angry with Mr. Goldstein. When Steve told me that Mr. Goldstein was coming to New York and wanted to visit with me, I hesitantly agreed. I remember telling him, "I want to meet the man who did this to you, and I want to kill him. I'm going to throw him off of our terrace!"

Mr. Goldstein and his wife visited Laura and me anyway. And instead of a violent or angry interchange, we discussed things over coffee and a Danish pastry ring. We asked them many questions, which they answered thoroughly. After a while, Mr. Goldstein pointed out prophecies in the Jewish Bible, and Laura was a little shocked to see that I was actually very curious to know more. What he said seemed to be some key to the "freedom" I still yearned for.

My curiosity continued past that evening, and I surprised even myself when I agreed to start attending Bible study meetings in New York. I became a very conscientious student. Each week we were asked to prepare for the next lesson by reading a particular passage from the Scriptures. One week the assignment was to read the first letter of John in the New Testament, but I read the Gospel of John by mistake. I couldn't put it down.

Then, on the morning of September 29, 1975, I woke up at 4 A.M. and sat right up in bed. I saw the outline of a figure standing in the doorway of my bedroom. I couldn't see a face, but I knew it was Jesus. I was convinced that He was real and that I wanted Him in my life. God must have known that it would take a supernatural event like this for me to become a believer in Jesus. For at that moment, because of this miraculous vision, I knew that He was my Messiah. I knew the Truth, and finally I felt free.

I didn't tell Laura until later in the day. She was upset about the news. First her son and now her husband too! To compound things, a few days later our youngest son, Robbie, announced that he too was a believer. He hadn't wanted to say anything until I came to believe because he was afraid that it would be too traumatic for me. In Robbie's words, "I didn't think you could take another one."

But could Laura take all of her family members believing in Jesus? She was very stubborn and quite upset. Despite the impact of seeing her husband and both sons become believers, she kept reminding herself about how many people had been killed in the Holocaust. So many Jews had been brutally killed. How could she betray her upbringing, her heritage? I understood her struggle.

Then Laura, Robbie, and I were invited to see a movie called *The Hiding Place*. We watched this true story about a Christian woman and her family in Holland during the war. Laura just sat there sobbing through the entire picture. I remember her telling me: "It showed the suffering this woman went through, yet she kept her faith in God. It made me see that God was working during the Holocaust—through people like this dear woman. Because she believed in Jesus, she helped Jews. She had real reason to hope."

The next week, Laura accepted Jesus as her Messiah.

Having both of us commit our lives to our Messiah brought Laura and me closer together. We fell in love again in a whole new way. Our relationship truly blossomed. Four years later, Laura and I renewed our marriage vows. After thirty years together, we became united again—this time in God's presence, showing forth His faithfulness. My own words still ring in my ears: "In a world where promises are seldom kept and faithfulness is scorned, I stand here today to declare my love for my wife and my love for Jesus."

My relationship with Jesus gave me freedom in many areas of my life: I am freer of self, so I can love others more, and I am free of much of the pain and guilt from my past. And though the healing continues, I know the best is yet to come. We have the great promises of God to rely upon as we live our lives in Messiah. "Being confident of this, that he who began a good work in you will carry it on to completion until the day of Christ Jesus" (Philippians 1:6).

F red is retired from the U.S. Postal Service. He and Laura—still his bride after fifty-two years of marriage—now live in California. They have two grown sons, who between them have several masters degrees, and five grandchildren. For more information on the Wertheim family, please contact them by e-mail at laura.wertheim@gte.net.

9

MAN OF MY DREAMS

Margolyn Woods

Oh how quickly the world's glory passes away.
THOMAS À KEMPIS

I had a wonderful childhood in Southern California, but life became really exciting for me in college when I was named Rose Bowl Queen for the 1972 "Tournament of Roses." During my reign, I appeared on numerous television shows—the *Bob Hope Christmas Show,* the *Carol Burnett Show,* the *Flip Wilson Show*—and starred in the first television commercial for a brand-new product called the Polaroid camera.

After my year in the limelight, I knew that I wanted a career in show business. I got some exciting roles on shows like *Vegas* and *Eddie Capra Mysteries,* and I also became the spokesperson for another new product, Rose Milk Skin Care Cream. Things were happening fast. I had stars in my eyes, and my acting career seemed to skyrocket overnight.

At a dinner party one evening, I met a well-known film producer. After a blissful year of dating, we were married in a star-studded ceremony, with many celebrities in attendance. But our joy was short-lived. Marriage to a film producer was not at all as glamorous as I thought it would be—I was soon lonely, unfulfilled, and disillusioned. After several years, we divorced.

As difficult as the divorce was, I had great hopes that if I married someone who wasn't in show business, I would be perfectly happy. So my new search began.

After about a year and hundreds of blind dates, matchmaking friends set me up on a lunch date with Roy, a professional race-car driver. I knew right away that he was marriage material. He wanted to settle down, he wanted children, he was absolutely charming, and—best of all—he was not in show business.

Roy swept me off my feet. After a three-week whirlwind courtship, we ran off to Las Vegas. I hadn't planned to elope, but Roy's next race was in Le Mans, France, and he had to leave immediately. It sounded so romantic to elope and run off to France! So, I quickly said yes. We got married on the Vegas strip in a little pink chapel with a big sign that said *All Checks OK*. Not exactly what I had hoped for in a wedding, but our honeymoon in the south of France made up for it. It was a storybook romance. I had the man of my dreams, and this time I knew I would live happily ever after.

It sounded so romantic to elope and run off to France!

I willingly sacrificed my soaring career in show business for the promise of a perfect new life in the Midwest with my race-car driver. And life did, indeed, seem perfect. Our home was an incredible estate called "Out of Bounds," where my daily routine consisted of choosing a menu for the cook, doing a little volunteer work, and playing tennis. For a while, everything was a dream come true. We had everything money could buy, and our lives were filled with exotic trips and lots of love. It was a lifestyle I had only read about in romance novels.

But after several years of traveling on the race-car circuit with

Roy, I was ready to settle down. I thought that he was ready too, but when I asked him to give up racing, he said "Someday, but not now." When I brought up having children, I got the same answer. When I asked him to at least come home each evening to sit down to dinner with me, he reminded me how lucky I was to have him. His response took me by surprise. I thought that I'd done Roy a big favor by giving up my career and moving, and this is what I got in return!

I'm sure that people looking at our lives from the outside must have thought that we had everything. But by this time neither of us was very happy, and I clearly recognized the signs of a marriage in trouble because I'd been there before.

I thought that going to church might help. Although my life probably didn't reflect it, I assumed that I was a Christian. While I was growing up, I was in church almost every time the doors opened. I sang in the choir and was even part of the youth group. Then when I moved away from home, I stopped going. Now seemed like a good time to start again. But when I asked Roy to go to church, he just asked curtly, "On my golf day?"

During this troubled period, the Hartzog family befriended me. Larry Hartzog was our family attorney, and over time I had gotten to know his wife, Gretchen. On Sunday mornings, while Roy was off on a racetrack or a golf course, Larry and Gretchen came by to pick me up for church. Soon I was crying on Gretchen's shoulder for hours, telling her about my turmoil. She patiently listened to every word I said. Then she asked me if I had ever asked Jesus Christ to come into my life.

I couldn't believe what I was hearing. With all the time I had spent in church, I had never heard it said that to be a child of God, I had to take the first step and *ask* Jesus to enter the picture. Gretchen then asked if I would like to say a simple prayer doing just that. Well, my life sure wasn't working out very well with me in charge, so I agreed. What did I have to lose? I asked Jesus to please come in and make me the woman He wanted me to be and to please help my marriage.

Suddenly, as I sat there crying, a light came on. I instantly knew that I had been trying to fill a void in my life that only Jesus could fill. He was the one I had been searching for—the Man of my dreams. I had thought that accolades, a husband, money, and things would bring me fulfillment, but they never had. I'm fortunate, not because I was given the things that most people think will satisfy them, but because I learned that they don't.

As I began to study the Bible and spend time in prayer and in church, Roy moved further and further away from me. When I learned that he had been unfaithful, I knew that I had to leave this marriage too. Devastated at my second failure, I moved to Colorado, where with the help of friends, I slowly began to put my life back together. Although I prayed that Roy might come to know the peace and love I had found in my new relationship with Jesus, I never asked God to give Roy back to me. The pain of his infidelity was just too deep.

Knowing how angry I was with Roy, a friend suggested that I ask God to change my heart toward him. She said she was concerned that my anger might be in the way of something God had in mind for me. Letting go of my anger was very difficult for me. I felt justified in holding on to it, yet I also had a strong desire to please God. So, reluctantly but honestly, I prayed that God would change my heart toward Roy. In time, the pain diminished, and my anger slowly faded.

About a year later, there was a knock at my door. Roy was standing there, suitcase in hand, wanting to start over. Our divorce was already final, but with my anger toward him gone, I let him move back in. Things went well for a while, and I thought we would be able to work things out. We were starting over in a new town, and he seemed to like Colorado. I was even beginning to trust him again.

But life in the world's fast lane still had a hold on Roy, and one day when I came home, I found a note telling me that he had left. Once again I was completely shattered. I couldn't live through this again. Had I been a fool to let him back in?

A month later, I realized that I was pregnant. I had always wanted children—but not in these circumstances! At thirty-one, I had had two failed marriages, and now I was going to be a single parent. I was devastated. For the first two months, I felt terribly sorry for myself.

Then God opened my eyes to the world around me. I started staring into the face of every baby I saw, wondering if I was carrying a girl or a boy and if my baby was healthy. Finally, I got down on my knees and asked God to forgive me and to stay really close to me while I had this baby. I sold my home and moved to Maui, Hawaii, where Roy and I shared a condo as part of our divorce settlement.

But life in the world's fast lane still had a hold on Roy.

The first Sunday after I arrived, I visited a church. In the church bulletin was an announcement that a childbirth class was starting that evening, and I decided to attend. We went around the room introducing ourselves and sharing why we had chosen this particular childbirth method. When it was my turn, I broke down and told these total strangers my entire life's story. They were wonderful. Today, I am so thankful for that group of Christian couples, who literally put their arms around me and helped me through one of the most devastating times in my life.

About six months later, there was another knock at my door. It was Roy again, suitcase in hand, wanting to start over. This time, my friends encouraged me to let him stay. And, boy, were those Christian husbands ready for him! They befriended him without judgment. They picked him up to play golf, they took him to play tennis, and they invited him to their homes. Roy saw that these men were different from any others he had spent time with. They had a "high" in their lives without drugs or expensive toys, and they had incredible respect for their wives and families.

Roy even attended church with me, and one day when our pastor asked if there was anyone who wanted to give his life over to Jesus Christ, my husband said yes.

If anyone had told me that I would not only forgive my husband, but also fall in love with him all over again, I would never have believed it. But with God nothing is impossible. With God as the foundation in our lives, Roy and I now have a wonderful marriage, and there is joy and peace in our home.

Our priorities have completely changed. Our life goal now is not to have all the world offers, but to have our children, family, and friends know God as intimately and fully as we know Him. We want to do for others what our church friends did for us—lead them to the life-changing love of Jesus.

Margolyn lives in Edmond, Oklahoma, with her husband, Roy, and three of their five children. She is a popular speaker at women's retreats and conferences across the country and the author of seven books. You can contact her at margolyn@mmcable.com.

10

FREE TO FORGIVE

Kitty Chappell

Children begin by loving their parents;
as they grow older they judge them;
sometimes they forgive them.
OSCAR WILDE

When I was fourteen years old, I decided to shoot my father.

I believed that it was the only way my mom, my younger brother and sister, and I could be free of him. He had threatened that if we ever told anyone that he physically abused us, he would kill us and plead temporary insanity. "I'll get away with it because my community will never convict me," he would state calmly. Since he was well liked and respected in our little town of Texarkana, Texas, we knew that no one would believe our word over his. So I decided that the next time he threatened us, I would some-how get the gun from him, pull the trigger, and end our misery.

One day, I was invited to church. Surprisingly, my father let me go. I couldn't believe what I heard when the minister read from John 3:16 in the Bible: "For God so loved the world that he gave his one and only Son, that whoever believes in him shall not perish but have eternal life."

I had heard about Jesus from my maternal grandmother, who was a devout Christian. I always felt safe in her home because of the peace and love there. But my earthly father didn't love me, so how could I expect a heavenly father to love me? And how could I trust a God who says that He loves me and yet lets my own father hurt me? Besides my doubts, I knew that I was undeserving, especially since I harbored the evil plan to kill my father. How could God love somebody like me, much less forgive me? Nevertheless, I deeply longed for God's love.

The minister went on to explain that no one deserves God's love and forgiveness. It is a gift. He read again from the Bible, this time Ephesians 2:8–9: "For it is by grace you have been saved, through faith…it is the gift of God—not by works."

Then a strange thing happened. The minister stopped, looked up from his old black Bible, and said, "*Whoever* has to include *you* because God is not a liar!" I was stunned. Then it had to be true. A God *that* loving wouldn't deliberately leave someone out, so His invitation had to include me.

The only thing I couldn't do was to forgive him for destroying all of our lives. That was asking too much.

As I prayed quietly in my heart, God's love entered my life. It felt as if He washed away all my sin and replaced it with an amazing peace. That day I became the child of a perfect father—my new heavenly Father—who promised never to leave me or forsake me, no matter what.

At home, however, things only got worse as Dad's abuse became more frequent. I was able to bear it because Jesus had begun to transform me, and I responded differently to the same horrible circumstances. Instead of planning to kill Dad, I began praying for him and treating him with more respect. The only thing I couldn't do was to forgive him for destroying all of our lives. That was asking too much.

When I was nineteen, we went on a rare family outing to a state park. Dad took Mom for a walk in the woods while my brother and sister and I played with our cousins. A short time later we heard screams. As a crowd gathered, I saw Mom run from the woods, stumbling toward me with blood streaming down the side of her face. A familiar feeling of terror and anger engulfed me as my mother sobbed out her story of how Dad had become angry and beaten her on the head with a rock. Moments later Dad appeared. He stated calmly that Mom was hysterical and that she had simply fallen.

That was when we knew that we had to get away or we would never survive. But how? After her wounds had healed somewhat, Mom asked Dad if she could visit her sister in California to recuperate. Dad happily let her go—alone.

School started shortly after Mom went to her sister's. This was my second year as secretary to the local elementary school. Midmorning the phone rang—it was Mom.

"Hi, Mom!" I said, delighted to hear her voice.

She cut me short. "Kitty, check your sister and brother out of school and come home immediately," she whispered into the phone. "We are going to California, and we've got to get out of here fast before your dad catches us. Hurry!"

"But I thought you were still in Ca…" I stammered.

"Your aunt and cousin drove me here. They're going to help us. Hurry!"

Suddenly, I stood at a crossroads. I knew we couldn't let anyone know where we were going for fear that Dad would find us. Still, I couldn't help but think of my dear friends. I would have to leave them all suddenly without even saying good-bye. But how could my family make it without me? Mom had only a fourth-grade education, and she didn't know how to drive. I loved my family more than life itself. I would rather die than abandon them.

"Okay, Mom. I'll be there as fast as I can," I said.

I called my little sister out of class and then rushed to my brother's school and picked him up. With pounding hearts, we packed all we could into our family car, met the others, and fled nonstop to California. I was terrified all the way and kept looking in the rearview mirror, expecting to see Dad barreling down upon us at any moment.

My father did find us, just as he had always said he would. He convinced my mother that he had changed, and she and my brother and sister moved back home. Not long after, in the middle of the night, he proceeded with his premeditated plan: He took a hammer and, repeatedly and methodically, beat my mother in the head until he was sure she was dead. Mom barely survived.

The state of Texas charged my father with premeditated attempted murder, and when Dad finally came to trial, he pled temporary insanity, just as he had said he would. As a basis for this plea, the defense attorneys accused Mom and me of being prostitutes in our home. They said that our immoral behavior had prompted my father's action. Who wouldn't have believed that kind-looking man sitting on the stand, tears streaming down his face as he lied about coming home one evening and finding his wife in bed with another man? And how it broke his heart to learn that his lovely daughter was a prostitute? The courtroom was packed, and Mom and I were humiliated beyond belief. It was one of the darkest times in my life.

My father was ultimately convicted of attempted premeditated murder and sent to prison for three and a half years. We were free, at least for a while. But were we?

I was still a prisoner because I refused to forgive my father. I argued with God. *I know You tell us that we must forgive, but I don't want to forgive my father. I hate what he has done to us. I want him to hurt—to be as miserable as he made us.* But after continually battling these overwhelming feelings, one day I finally gave in and said, *Lord, You know how much I don't want to forgive my father, but*

I do want to obey You. I want to please You more than I want to hang on to my hate and resentment, and I want to be free of this. It's eating me up inside. Would You please help me to change?

It was some time later—weeks, maybe a month—I'm not sure. But I do remember exactly how it happened. One day I was suddenly overtaken with an overwhelming desire to forgive my father.

I was cleaning house one Saturday morning, humming a song as I finished dusting. As I turned to replace a delicate figurine on the shelf, I realized that I was filled with pure compassion for my father. I had not even been thinking about him. I was enjoying our new life of freedom. This glorious and strong desire to wipe away the bitterness toward my father happened so quickly that I just broke down crying. I heard

I was still a prisoner because I refused to forgive my father.

my voice say to the empty room, "Dad, I really do want to forgive you—and I do. I forgive you for everything."

At that moment, my heart broke free from its heavy burden of resentment, and my spirit soared heavenward on wings of forgiveness. Once again, God had heard and answered my prayer, and a miracle happened.

My father was released from prison a year early because of "good behavior." We lived in fear that he would come back to us, and we jumped every time the doorbell or the phone rang. But thankfully, he never showed up again.

One day, more than three decades after I had last seen him, I received a letter from Dad saying that he had remarried and had a son. He asked me to forgive him for the past. It took me three days to compose my response. In my letter, I listed all of the heartaches he had caused me. "Dad, I'm pleased you ask my forgiveness," I wrote. "And though I forgave you years ago, I list your wrongs only to show the extent of my forgiveness. The one whose forgiveness you should ask, however, is God. You see, Dad, I can forgive you for the wrongs you've done to me, but only God can forgive you of your sins."

After almost a year of correspondence by mail, Dad pleaded with me, again by letter, to visit him. "Your brother Chuck brought his family to see me. Isn't it time for you and your sister, Chris, to visit me as well?"

My husband and I, along with Chris and her husband, Everett, decided to respond to Dad's request, and we made the three-hour drive to his home. My heart pounded as we stepped into his house. *What can possibly happen after all these years?* I thought. *What will I feel about him? Why am I doing this?*

Dad appeared to be just as cunning as when I had last seen him. I suspected that his plea for forgiveness had been merely a way to reestablish contact. Only God knew the truth, but this time I felt sorry for Dad. He was an old man trying to snatch a few precious moments with the children he had previously abused.

I recall sitting there in the living room with Dad, his second wife, our half-brother, and his wife. *This has to be a miracle,* I thought. *To sit here in the presence of the man I once hated and feared so much that I planned to kill him and now feel nothing but compassion and peace.* As I talked with my father that evening, I knew that I was the one who was really free—free to go on with my life.

Sadly, Dad never found God's forgiveness and was never truly set free. Almost a year after our visit, in one of his mad rages, he murdered his second wife and then shot himself.

This miracle of forgiveness was possible for me only because one day over forty years earlier, as I was on a path to destruction, I met God—and it changed the direction of my life forever.

Kitty has been married to her husband, Jerry, for forty-three years. They have two children and one granddaughter. Kitty is a freelance writer, and she also speaks to Christian Women's Clubs and other women's functions for Stonecroft Ministries. Kitty and Jerry reside in Gilbert, Arizona.

11

FOREVER AND EVER, AMEN

Randy Travis

*I have learned the secret of living in every situation,
whether it is with a full stomach or empty, with plenty or little.*
PAUL OF TARSUS

I was born Randy Traywick on May 4, 1959, and I grew up on a farm in the little town of Marshville, North Carolina. We weren't wealthy, but we weren't poor—some might even call us hillbillies. My family raised cattle, and my daddy, also a contractor, had always wanted to be a country music singer. Since he never got to fulfill his own dream, he encouraged us to try, so I learned to play the guitar and sing. When I was nine, my brother Ricky and I started performing together in clubs.

I attended church some as a kid, but as they say in the South, "it didn't take." My mom was a great example of "turning the other cheek," but I couldn't see it. I had a terrible temper, and I grew up fighting with everybody around me. I fought so much that I would have become a professional fighter—if it weren't for the fact that I lost every fight.

I drifted way off course in my teenage years. To say that I got on the wrong road was an understatement. There wasn't even a road where I ended up. In my case, it started mainly because of peer pressure. I saw what the kids around me were doing, so I gave in to "drink this" and "smoke that." By the age of eleven, I was smoking cigarettes and marijuana. By thirteen, I was abusing every substance I could get, and by the time I was fifteen, my life revolved around drugs, drinking, and fighting. I dropped out of school and took a construction job. My substance abuse led to crime, and I was arrested for high-speed chases, vehicle theft, assault, and breaking and entering. I totaled four cars, a couple of motorcycles, and even a horse and buggy. I was on a first-name basis with the entire Marshville police force.

To say that I got on the wrong road was an understatement. There wasn't even a road where I ended up.

The last time I appeared in court was in 1976. I was seventeen years old and looking at five years in prison. That's where I would have ended up if it hadn't been for Elizabeth Hatcher, the owner of a club where I was singing. The first time she heard me sing, she immediately believed that I could truly make something of myself. She went to the courthouse that day and convinced the judge to let me go. Elizabeth took responsibility and told the judge that I had a full-time job and would quit drugs and alcohol. She conveyed to the judge that she believed in me and that I really did want to change. That was the truth—at that point I knew I had to. I was so low there was nowhere else to go.

The judge listened to Elizabeth, looked at me, and finally said, "Son, I'm going to let you go one more time, but if you ever come before me again, bring your toothbrush, because you're staying."

Elizabeth started grooming me as a country singer. I saw something in her that I wasn't used to seeing. Her lifestyle was totally opposite from the selfish, reckless way I lived. She did things for other people all the time, not because she had to, but just because that's who she was. Most amazing was how calmly she responded to my outbursts of anger. If we got into an argument, she wouldn't fight back. Her example made me want to change. For the first time, I seriously considered asking God to help.

In 1981, after a very unhappy marriage, Elizabeth got a divorce, sold her club, and we moved to Nashville. Lib got a job managing a club; I was hired as a dishwasher, part-time cook, and later on as a singer. There was no quick career breakthrough; in fact, over the course of ten years, every record company in town turned me down two or three times. But I never once got discouraged. We changed my name to Randy Ray and just kept plugging.

After twelve years of singing in clubs to meager crowds, I became an "overnight success."

During that time, I was trying to be a better person inside, not because other people told me to, but because I was ready to. Looking at myself, all I saw was a poor excuse for a human being, and I knew I needed help. So I started reading the Bible and watching the preachers on TV. Years later, Lib and I began attending church, and through time I came to know Him personally.

But for me it was a slow process—not just a moment in time when God knocked me over and instantly transformed every aspect of my life. First, I recognized my need for Him, and then very slowly I watched myself change from a rebellious, violent kid into a peaceful, contented man. By the time I was twenty-five, I had completely given up drugs and alcohol. The only part of me that hadn't changed was my shyness and temper. But, I knew that God wasn't done with me.

In 1985, Lib finally convinced Warner Brothers Records to give me a chance. First they changed my last name to Travis and tested two singles, one of which was "On the Other Hand." It became my first number-one hit. After twelve years of singing in clubs to meager crowds, I became an "overnight success."

I began my career walking around like a deer caught in the

headlights. Although I was scared to death, I experienced peace and contentment, with a strength that surely came from God.

By 1990 our love for God and each other had grown, and I asked Elizabeth to change her name as well—to Travis. God had put us together, and Lib went from being my best friend and teacher to my manager to my soul mate.

One Sunday about ten years after I first met God, while attending our little church in Ashland City, I finally decided to take the next step. After the service that day, I walked straight up to our pastor and said, "Dan, I need to get baptized." He seemed shocked. He stepped back, took a breath, and said, "Well, okay…but I want to sit down and talk with you first."

So that afternoon, Pastor Dan Harless and his wife, Jane, came over to our house, and we talked about why I felt that it was time to get baptized. Jesus had become very important to me, and I needed to make a public confession of my faith. That evening both Elizabeth and I were baptized. That was the day I personally experienced God. I was filled with a sense of peace and assurance that I still feel in my soul today. It was a public declaration of faith, and it will always be the reminder that God changed the direction of my life.

I can't tell you that I never do anything wrong, because I still have a terrible temper, and it causes me to say things that I regret. I still make mistakes, but now I know that there is forgiveness with Jesus.

I wanted to make a living in the music business, and I'm so grateful for the success that God has granted me. But real success can't be measured in terms of fame, fortune, and awards. I've known people who seem to have it all, but in reality they were some of the unhappiest people I've ever met. To me, true success in life has come to mean peace and contentment. These come only from God—and they come forever and ever.

Amen.

R andy is one of the most popular artists in the history of country music, having received three Grammy awards, five CMA
awards, eight ACM awards, and ten American Music awards. His
eleven albums and CDs have sold 21 million copies. He and Lib
live in Nashville, Tennessee.

12

THE PYRAMID FLIPPED OVER

David Erwin

The Christian ideal has not been tried and found wanting.
It has been found difficult and left untried.
G. K. CHESTERTON

In *The Varieties of Religious Experience,* William James uses the pyramid as a metaphor for the human mind. He says that when a religious experience—a miracle, epiphany, or revelation—occurs, the pyramid-mind flips over, as it were, onto a new base. The mind still works the same, but it now sees, understands, and believes differently. The day I met God, my pyramid flipped over.

For more than thirty years, I searched for truth in special knowledge, the arcane, the occult, and other spiritual practices hidden from the world at large. Believing that I was spiritually enlightened, I leaned only on my own understanding and cleverness. I was like a drowning man who, in desperation and with his last ounce of strength, manages to push his hand above the water in the chance that someone or something will save him.

Spiritual issues were rarely discussed while I was growing up, although Dad was a Freemason and Mom was involved in the women's counterpart, Eastern Star. When the name of Jesus was used in our home, it was not out of reverence. However, I did sing in the church choir with my mother, and I developed a deep love for music.

When I was in seventh grade, my parents bought me a brand-new silver Bach trumpet. They encouraged me by paying for lessons, and I became a fairly proficient player. While at college on a music scholarship, I was introduced to the music of the Mahavishnu Orchestra, featuring guitarist John McLaughlin, who had played with Miles Davis. John was a devotee of Sri Chinmoy, an Eastern spiritual guru whose writings on oneness and meditation greatly appealed to me.

I ordered some pamphlets, began to meditate, and soon discovered a real avenue to the spiritual realm. I believed that there was unlimited potential within me that I could realize through gurus, gods, meditation, and magic. Just like most of my musical heroes in the seventies, I believed that drugs promised a mind-expanding way to enlightenment, so in addition to drinking alcohol, I smoked marijuana daily and eventually experimented with LSD and cocaine.

I ordered some pamphlets, began to meditate, and soon disovered a real avenue to the spiritual realm.

In 1980, I had a miserable breakup with my first real girlfriend. I was playing in a jazz ensemble at the time, and the trombone player came to comfort me. He brought a Bible and told me about the gospel. I was polite but not interested. I believed that I was moving beyond a need for Jesus. In fact, I had just changed my major from music to Eastern philosophy.

About that same time, another musician gave me a book about Scientology. I had been a great fan of jazz pianist Chick Corea and bassist Stanley Clarke, and I knew that both credited Scientology founder L. Ron Hubbard on their albums. It seemed plausible to me that their outstanding musical abilities had something to do with being involved in Scientology. If it worked for them, maybe it would work for me.

In 1981, I moved to Germany to play in a show band. While traveling with the band, I learned that there were many Scientology centers there, and during a break from the tour, I signed up for a series of classes. Eventually the classes got so expensive that I couldn't afford them, so they offered to put me on staff in trade. I stopped using drugs and alcohol, but I was not allowed to take outside jobs or express my opinions, which were viewed as "other intentions." I was no longer motivated to play the trumpet, and music no longer brought me joy. After more than a year, I felt like a slave.

One cold night in 1984, with financial help from my parents, I grabbed a cab to the airport, jumped on the plane, and flew back to the States, with nothing except my horn in tow. My music career seemed doomed, and my spiritual self was in ruins. I had just turned twenty-five years old, and I still didn't have any answers.

After having played in all the major cities in Europe, I couldn't bear to return to my small, dying hometown or another harsh Kansas winter. So, again with the help of my parents, I went to Key West, Florida—a place where the weather was warm, the drinks were cold, and I could start over again in anonymity. I managed to support myself through a series of jobs in radio. In Key West, it was easier to get cocaine than to catch fish, and I was soon using it more heavily than I had before. It was an empty existence.

Without friends or family, I felt trapped and alone, so in October of 1986, yet again with the financial help of my parents, I went to Denver to live with an old college friend, Tim, and his parents. Within a year, I had a job at a major radio station. Tim and his family were committed Christians, but I couldn't understand their faith in their God. Over the next few years, I investigated more New

Age practices. I read every book by Edgar Cayce and the entire Carlos Castaneda series. I looked into astrology and read many books on alien intervention. Finally, I settled on Zen Buddhism as my personal philosophy.

In the last few months of 1989, the Denver economy was sagging, and so was my radio career. I had to do something else. After months of traveling and performing, I moved to Atlanta, where I got a job producing radio commercials and playing trumpet in a rock band. At that studio I met a man who invited me to attend a Gnostic mass. He was a practicing member of the Ordo Templi Orientis, a higher order of freemasonry that practices magic—ceremonial magic, not the card-trick kind. During the ceremony, as the high priest practiced divination, I witnessed a fantastic event: A gale gust of wind swept through the closed room. That convinced me beyond any doubt that the world of unseen forces was very real.

During the ceremony, as the high priest practiced divination, I witnessed a fantastic event.

When you start to know the secrets of the universe, it's hard to share them with just anybody. After years of searching for enlightenment in the dark side of the spirit world, all my study had left me with only profound feelings of loneliness, hopelessness, and emptiness. I was an outcast, a prisoner of my own device. I was sick of the band scene and not at all fulfilled doing studio work. King Solomon once said, "Meaningless! Meaningless! Everything is meaningless!" That was absolutely true for me.

Something had to change, and for me there was only one place left to go—to the center of New Age thought, where good men die like dogs, children shoot each other for bags of money, and even the cops are afraid. I moved to L.A.

I stayed with friends and started to get work producing radio commercials. After only a few weeks, I met a single parent who openly shared her life with me. I believed that I could help her and her daughter by using the "superior knowledge" I had acquired. I also felt that this was what I needed to fill the ever-growing void inside of me. So we got married. The marriage lasted exactly nine-teen months, and the divorce was by far the most painful experi-ence of my entire life.

By April of 1997, all I had was my music and a very few caring friends. I was performing in a club in Hollywood, and I invited a friend, Anna, and her husband, Scott, to one of my shows. Anna ended up asking me to audition for her church choir. I had sung in many choirs, so I auditioned. To my surprise, I met people who showed me love, and for an entire year I heard the message of Jesus preached every Sunday.

Then I met Conrad.

Conrad was my sixty-five-year-old neighbor. He and I passed each other in the parking garage every morning for almost two years without ever exchanging more than the requisite "How ya doin'?" and "Fine, thanks." Then one day, out of the blue, he stopped and announced, "I just found out that I have fourth-stage metastasized prostate cancer, and they've given me six months to live. The cancer has spread to my bones and my PSA (Prostate Serum Antigen) count is 419, which makes me too far gone for chemo or radiation."

He went on to say that he belonged to a small, Messianic Jewish congregation, that he was on their prayer list, that he also prayed, and that he would appreciate my prayers as well. At that, a wall went up. I remember thinking, *Yeah, whatever.* Still, his words opened up the possibility of a friendship.

For a couple of months, Conrad and I got together once a week to "philosophize," and then in March I took a vacation to New Zealand. When I returned, I fully expected Conrad not to be there. But he was, and he actually looked quite a bit better. I remember being amazed at how at peace he seemed to be.

I continued to work sporadically as a sound editor for films and

TV, but I became more and more disgruntled with my chosen career in the "business we call show." Finally, I just gave up. I quit everything, even choir. I was broken financially, emotionally, and spiritually.

That July, all I did in the afternoons was sit by the pool. When Conrad saw me reading a book called *The Hiram Key-Freemasonry and the Secret Scrolls of Jesus,* he initiated a series of question-and-answer sessions. "So, Dave," he began, "who do you say that Jesus was?" But I was the one with the questions. Conrad could argue from any paradigm I chose, and he always answered my questions with a biblical reference. I was astounded at how knowledgeable he was, and I couldn't help but take it all in.

Toward the end of July, Conrad went back to the Veterans Administration Hospital to get an MRI and an update on his condition. His PSA count had dropped from 419 to 9. Had he been misdiagnosed? Was it a miracle? Although he still had cancer, he had been given a stay of execution. I couldn't rationalize away what had happened. I really felt that God was trying to show me something and that I had better pay attention.

My faithful friends Randy and Lara had been urging me to rejoin the choir, and when I showed up at the choir retreat at Capistrano Beach, everybody welcomed me back with open arms. I didn't feel worthy of their friendship and love. I noticed how they interacted with one another and with their kids and how much they prayed and loved God. I remember thinking, *I wonder if I could have a life like that?*

Sunday morning before we left, we had communion, and at that service the coin finally dropped into my spiritual slot. Everything I had orchestrated through my own cleverness disintegrated, and everything that Conrad had been telling me about the Bible and the plan of God suddenly made sense. The pyramid flipped over onto a new base, and I was absolutely convicted. At the age of forty, I accepted the gift of salvation through Jesus

Christ, the Son of the Creator of the universe. That was the day I met God.

The coin finally dropped into my spiritual slot.

Over the next few weeks, Conrad and I talked more about our lives. It was electric. Conrad had been a Buddhist for more than fifteen years, he knew all about Edgar Cayce and the Castaneda books I had read, and he had a brother who had been heavily into Scientology, so he had a working knowledge of that as well. Conrad had been a tarot card reader and an astrologer. He had been deep into ceremonial magic—not the card-trick kind. And, he had been forty when he came to know Jesus as the God-man, Savior, and Lord.

The coin finally dropped into my spiritual slot.

A true mentor, Conrad presented me with a copy of a study Bible. Because I was familiar with the spirit realm, I recognized the Bible as a supernatural book, not just stories for the simple-minded. And I certainly recognized the truth of Ephesians 6:12: "For our struggle is not against flesh and blood, but against the rulers, against the authorities, against the powers of this dark world and against the spiritual forces of evil in the heavenly realms."

Through His grace and in His time, God revealed Himself to me: through the trombone player in college; through my friend's parents in Denver; through the friends in the choir who loved me; and, most of all, through His messenger, Conrad, who had walked a similar path to faith twenty years earlier.

At times, certain images remind me of the poor choices I made in the past. But I am free of the lure of the dark side of New Age spiritualism, and I know that I am a new creature—one who is truly enlightened.

Dave is a professional sound designer for film and television in Los Angeles, and he still sings in the choir. He would like to give a special "God Bless You" to Lara and Randy, Anna and Scott, Nancy and Richard, Patt and Stan, and—especially—Conrad.

13

BEATING THE ODDS

Chuck Obremski

*Snatching the eternal out of the desperately fleeting
is the great magic trick of human existence.*
TENNESSEE WILLIAMS

T o say I had rough edges would be an understatement. I grew up in Pittsburgh, Pennsylvania, at a time when residents took pride in its reputation for hard drinking and riotous living. In fact, in the sixties a sportswriter covering a Steelers game wrote this about my hometown:

> Pittsburgh's two favorite beverages are a shot and a beer. It's the only place where I've been that canaries sing bass and restaurants serve broken leg of lamb.

Our family lived on the south side in the shadows of the steel mills, where my stepfather went to work after he dropped out of high school. His father had once owned a boxing clinic, so it was not uncommon for us to wake up to the sound of Dad working out his aggressions on a speed bag in the basement. But the punching bag was not always enough. Sometimes he pounded on my mom and us kids too.

By the time I was fifteen, I was sick of Dad beating up on Mom. One night at dinner, I jumped up and grabbed him—in hindsight, not the wisest move. He picked me up and threw me through the screen door into the front yard. Flat on my back, I looked up and saw that Mom had pushed him up against the wall and was holding a knife to his throat. It was one of those lasting impressions.

To escape the violence at home, I took my own anger to the football field, where violence was an accepted part of the game. I became the only person in the history of our high school to be thrown out of a scrimmage for hitting too hard. What I couldn't vent on the field, I drowned in booze.

I became the only person in the history of our high school to be thrown out of a scrimmage for hitting too hard.

One night, some of my football buddies and I went out drinking and carousing after a game. We drove home in separate cars. The driver in my buddies' car made a crazy sharp turn, and two of them fell out. Both died instantly when they were struck by oncoming traffic. That incident affected me deeply, and it should have been a turning point in my life. But it wasn't. Instead of sobering up and changing, I just drank more to deaden my pain.

I also had a girlfriend on whom to dump all my anxiety. I started dating Linda early in high school. She was beautiful, smart, and two years older than me. I was quite smitten. She stood out because she was so different from me. We were living proof that opposites attract. Unlike me, she knew that her parents really loved her. However, unfortunately for her but fortunately for me, she was attracted to bad boys.

Two and a half years after we started dating, Linda got pregnant, and against the advice of our families, we got married. I was eighteen and she was twenty when our daughter was born. Angry at my predicament, I started to hate life. I dropped out of college, worked two jobs, and like everyone else around me, masked my misery with shots and Iron City Beer—Pittsburgh's number-one brew.

It wasn't long before our marriage began to deteriorate. In fact, its demise seemed inevitable. But in one last-ditch effort to make it work, Linda and I packed up and moved to Southern California, the place my friends referred to as "the land of quakes and flakes." We were willing to try anything to save face and stick together.

Broke and struggling to survive, we were in for a culture shock. Not long after we arrived, we learned how really strange some Californians are. We were window-shopping at the mall one day when a man and a woman stopped us and the man said to me, "Fred, how have you been?"

I just looked at him.

"Well, what did you do to your hair?" he asked. "It used to be blond and now it's brown. In fact, your eyes are brown and they used to be blue. Do you have those contacts in there?"

Dumbfounded, I said, "Hey, man, my name's not Fred. It's Chuck."

The man turned to his wife and said, "Can you believe that? This guy even changed his name." And they walked away.

As bizarre as California seemed, we still hoped for a fresh start. However, we soon realized that no matter where we went, we took our problems with us. Nothing changed. Financially, our only hope for any kind of a future was for me to finish college. So I enrolled at Cal State Fullerton with a major in criminology. Hard and cynical about people, I figured that society was messed up. Why not study it? So I pursued my degree and worked while Linda stayed at home with our daughter. I just kept busy and continued to hate life.

Linda wasn't any happier. Stuck in our little apartment with the baby and three thousand miles away from her family, she was so lonely and miserable that she kept a packed suitcase by the door. But she never had the nerve to leave. The only reason we stayed together was because everybody had told us that our marriage would never work. We didn't really care if we were miserable; out of pure stubbornness and pride, we were going to make our marriage last just to prove them wrong.

The only reason we stayed together was because everybody had told us that our marriage would never work.

Finally, bored and tired of being poor, Linda decided to go back to work. She had been an executive secretary back home, so it didn't take her long to find a job. She went to work for a mechanical contracting company, and there she met some people she found very intriguing.

As she got to know her coworkers, Linda saw that everything about their lives—their marriages, their families, their actions—was much different than ours. They knew how to love, forgive, and really talk to one another. We had none of that in our relationship. The single word that would sum up the difference between them and us was *peace*—an absence of turmoil—a wonderful quality we recognized but didn't really understand.

At lunch one of the girls in the office started telling Linda about the personal relationship she had with Jesus. Fascinated, Linda told me about it when she got home.

"Oh, gee…that's great. Somebody knows Jesus," I said.

Ignoring my sarcasm, she replied, "No…I mean…she said that she knows Jesus and that there was a time in her life when she asked God to forgive her and invited Him to be Lord of her life." I remained the cynic, but as time went on, Linda became convinced that these people were for real.

Then one day in my debate class the topic for discussion was the cause of evil in society. Was it due to people's heredity or their environment? A religious couple in class stood up together, and the guy said, "As far as debating the cause of evil, we could go on all night. But there is one thing that we've discovered in our own lives, and that is that Jesus Christ makes a difference. Jesus can overcome whatever background you have. Whatever family situations, whatever the heredity or environment problems, Jesus not only forgives sin, but He also gives you an abundant life."

I'd about had it with all this Jesus stuff! It was everywhere I turned—at home and now at school. So I yelled at them, "Shut up and sit down! This isn't the place for that religious stuff. Take it to your religion or philosophy class." The class broke into applause as if to say, "Right on! Somebody has to shut up these fanatics." But as I left, something was bothering me, and I didn't tell Linda about the class.

Shortly after that, Linda called me with great news. The people where she worked wanted to interview me for a job. The pay was better, the benefits were great, the hours worked well around my school schedule, and we could drive to work together. It was ideal.

I had never seen anything like the work ethic at that place. Employees would actually call vendors and say, "You haven't billed us yet for materials we bought two months ago." Then somebody would make a call and say, "Hey, you paid us double. We owe you a refund." These kinds of calls floored me. Where I came from, if somebody forgot to send you an invoice, it was a sign from God that you didn't have to pay. Here, it was an error that had to be corrected.

These people really walked their talk about God. What they believed affected the way they lived. They weren't like most religious people I knew who went to church and acted holy on Sunday but behaved like the rest of us Monday through Saturday. There was so much depth to them that I couldn't wait to find out more. My cynical attitude toward my fellow man was slowly beginning to melt.

When Bob at work asked me to a steak barbecue one Sunday, I jumped at the chance. In fact, I accepted before he sprang it on me that he and his wife wanted Linda and me to meet them at church first and then go to their house afterwards. Well, I couldn't turn down a good steak. And I figured I'd gone to church before and survived. One more time wasn't going to kill me.

Sunday ended up being rather interesting. It was the first time I'd ever gone to a church where somebody picked up the Bible and explained things so they made some sense. However, I didn't want to give Bob the impression that I wanted to go back, so I kept a low profile.

When we got to Bob's house, the gals stayed inside while Bob and I started up the barbecue. Curiosity got the best of me, and while he was cooking, I blurted out, "Hey, let me ask you— What's with you? You drive me crazy, man. I've never met anybody like you. This has to be a joke."

"You mean…why am I the way I am?" Bob asked.

"Yeah," I replied.

"Because I'm a Christian."

Blowing a sigh of relief, "Whew, that's good. So am I," I said.

"Really? When did you become a Christian?" Bob asked.

Now I was thinking that this was a trick question. *Tread carefully*, I warned myself, not knowing how in the world to answer. Finally I blurted out, "We've gone to church off and on. We were married in the church. I was even baptized as a baby."

I looked over at Bob, and he had this look on his face like "No, that's not it." Talk about pressure. I mean, I was used to essays in college where you just keep talking, and the longer you talk, the more chance you have of getting something right. But it wasn't happening here.

Finally Bob asked, "Would you mind if I told you how a person becomes a Christian?"

Ready for any escape out of my misery, I said, "Sure."

"You know the verse in the Bible that says that all have sinned and fallen short of the glory of God?" he asked.

I nodded as if I really knew.

"Well, falling short is like when you're golfing and you putt, but the ball stops short of the hole," Bob said.

I golf, so I could relate to that. As good a person as I thought I was, I knew I wasn't perfect, and goodness is such a relative thing. Linda certainly didn't think I was as good as I thought I was! Bob continued on with other analogies as we finished up the steaks and took them inside.

In the weeks and months that followed, I thought about what we had discussed that day in Bob's backyard. And I recalled the words of that religious couple I had jumped all over in my debate class. Six months later, I even managed to find our old family Bible and began reading it. I wasn't ready to commit, just curious enough to investigate.

About one year later, Linda and I were at a banquet we had been invited to, and the speaker was telling us about Jesus. By this time, we'd heard the same thing, in different ways, many times. But that night something clicked, and I just gave up. I waved a white flag and said, *Okay, God, I surrender. I can't fight You any more. Your love is too compelling. I'm sick of who I've been. I don't understand all this, but I believe what You say. I want to know and trust Jesus to take over my life.* Unbeknownst to me, Linda came to the same conclusion. That night—February 16, 1978—we both met God.

After that night, Linda and I dramatically changed from the inside out. We both stopped drinking, and our marriage turned around. We beat the statistics—not out of pride, but out of real love for each other—and we recently celebrated our twenty-fifth wedding anniversary. We have three children, Dana, Ryan, and Krista, and one grandson, Luke. I know these many blessings are only because of what Jesus Christ has done in our lives. The Bible says that if man is in Christ, he is a new creature and that old things pass away and all things become new. We've seen that happen before our very eyes.

One thing that didn't change was my love for football, and God used it. He opened doors for me to be the chaplain of the Rams football team from 1984 to1986 and again from 1989 to 1994. After the Rams moved from Anaheim to St. Louis, another opportunity opened up, and I have been the chaplain of the Anaheim Angels baseball team since 1997.

Sure there are scars from our past, but we choose to look at all of them as examples of God's grace and something He can bring us from instead of dwelling on things that could hold us back.

I *was* a cynical product of my environment, but *now* I'm a product of grace!

Chuck is the owner of Horizon Heating and Air Conditioning in Orange County, California. He's been teaching an adult Sunday school class at Calvary Church, Santa Ana, since 1983 and is currently the chaplain of the Anaheim Angels.

14

DADDY DEAREST

Linda Hoeper

> *It doesn't matter who my father was;*
> *it matters who I remember he was.*
> ANNE SEXTON

I encountered God for the first time in 1957, when I was eight years old. But I really met Him at the bedside of my dying father in 1991, when I was forty-two years old.

When I was eight, I contracted a severe case of German measles. I had a dangerously high fever, and the doctor said that I was dying. I was hallucinating, and in my delirium, I saw a man with a beer bottle in his hand hiding behind the curtains in my bedroom. I told my mother repeatedly that this strange man was going to kill me. Then I sat straight up in bed, looked directly at her, and said in an extremely stern voice, "Mother, are you still in this hellhole? The angels are coming for me. I'm going home to be with Jesus."

All I remember is raising my arms as two angels above me stretched their arms toward me. I saw just their faces—they looked like the faces of children. I lifted my hands toward heaven and then collapsed. At that exact moment my fever broke, and almost immediately after I lay back down, I made a full recovery. From that day on I felt very special. God had sent two of His angels just for me, so clearly He had kept me here for a purpose.

My mother was the only believer in our family, and she raised all five of her children in church. When I was twelve, I was in church with my mom when a well-meaning adult dragged me down to the altar so I could commit my life to Jesus. They prayed—I mostly cried. I walked away confused, thinking that maybe if I could just be good enough, God would accept me. But nothing happened that day, and what I learned about Jesus in Sunday school had no real impact on my life as the years rolled by.

Dad lived by his own golden rule: "Whoever makes the gold, makes the rules."

In fact, I grew up hating my father.

Dad was a compulsive gambler—chasing after the next "big win" consumed him and all his time. He called gambling his second job, but in fact it was his only true passion. I could never count on anything growing up because I never knew if Dad would destroy our hopes and plans by coming home broke again.

Dad also lived by his own golden rule: "Whoever makes the gold, makes the rules." He believed only in himself, lived his life solely for his own pleasure, and never considered what was best for his family.

I hated my father not so much for the neglect and selfishness of his lifestyle, but because he wouldn't return the love of his wife and children. Every little girl yearns for the love of her father, and when she doesn't receive it, something inside her dies. My trust died at a very young age.

I firmly believed that I had to be in charge of my own life, and I learned to trust in my own ability to earn money and provide for myself. By the time I was fourteen, I had vowed that I would never live under the thumb of any man. I would make the "gold" and the "rules." As I grew into adulthood, I trusted more and more in myself. In a macabre sort of way, I became like my father.

Despite my lack of trust, when I was twenty-three, I met a wonderful man and decided to marry him. I even agreed to join his church. For some reason, church was the one area where I acquiesced in my husband's leadership. However, my desperate need to be in charge carried over into the other areas of our marriage. For the first twenty years, I wore the pants in our relationship.

Even though I attended church every Sunday, I was literally "in the pew without a clue." I repeated the prayers and sang the songs, but Jesus was not real to me. I was in charge of my own destiny— or so I thought.

Then, in the fall of 1991, when I was forty-two years old, my father was diagnosed with bone cancer. I had been alienated from him and didn't even know he was sick. He had been admitted to the hospital for treatment, but the doctors knew that he was dying. The best the doctors could do for him was to give him unlimited morphine for the pain. Ironically, one of the side effects of that much morphine is hallucination.

My mother called to ask me to visit my father in the hospital. He was seeing some very strange sights, and she didn't know what to do. I agreed only to meet with her and my youngest sister to talk about it. When we met, they told me that Dad had seen demons and heard them screaming at him about the flames of hell. And he had seen his eighteen-month-old grandson hanging dead in the corner where the hospital television was mounted to the wall. They were scared and didn't know what to do. I could hardly believe my ears.

My mind raced as I drove home that night. *I don't care about him! What do I do? Can I handle this? What are these demons? Do I have to go? What am I supposed to do? My struggle continued throughout the night.*

Finally, I decided to go see him.

When I walked into Dad's hospital room the next evening, what I saw sent chills up my spine. This man, whom I grew up hating and even fearing, was tied to the bed rails so he wouldn't rip out the IVs and try to escape from the room. He looked so fragile, so frightened lying there in that hospital bed. *Was this the man I had been so bitter toward for so long? Could I hate this man?* I saw my father differently that night, and my heart broke. He was so helpless....

I began to ask Dad about the things he had been seeing in his room. He told me about the flames and smoke that filled his room and the slime that hung over his bed. He described his sensation that his bed was standing on end at the edge of the bottomless pit as the ceiling opened up to an incredibly bright light. As he was speaking, his eyes widened, and a look of terror crossed his face. I knew he was seeing something that was very real to him.

"Dad, what are you seeing?" I asked.

He whispered that it was a disjointed demon pointing his bony finger right at him.

"How do you know it's a demon?" I asked.

His answer almost made me laugh. "Because it has a sign around its neck that spells out the word: *d-e-m-o-n.*"

Here was a man who, in all his sixty-three years, had been in church only to attend a few weddings and funerals. Now God was forcing him to see the result of the horrible choices he had made during his life. I went home that night with the frightening realization that my father was bound for hell.

The next morning I called a new pastor at our church and told him about my father's spiritual condition. He didn't know me and had never met my father, but he promised to visit him that evening. On my way to the hospital, I stopped by my mother's home to retrieve a little black Bible I'd been given when I was ten years old. It was the first time in years that I'd thought about that Bible.

I did things that day I never would have dreamed of, much less done. I spent the entire day with my dad, reading the Psalms to him from my little black Bible, wiping away imaginary slime from above his head, and waving my arms where he thought he saw a demon to show him that there was nothing to fear.

The entire time I read to Dad, I had the oddest sensation that I was holding something—a weapon?—in my right hand, when in fact, I was holding a Bible in my left hand. It was as if I were waging war against the forces of evil for the soul of my father. I asked Dad if he believed in God, and he answered, "I believe God is in everything and everything is God." My heart sank. His answer wasn't good enough.

> *It was as if I were waging war against the forces of evil for the soul of my father.*

That evening the pastor came as promised and told my dad the most beautiful story of Jesus that I had ever heard. He talked about how people try to work their way to God, but to no avail. He told Dad that the only way to God is through Jesus Christ, who reaches down to us and does for us what we can never do for ourselves—make us good enough for Him. I was mesmerized. My father listened intently to everything the pastor had to say, but he never said whether or not he agreed with what he heard.

I walked the pastor to the elevator, and when I returned, it was just Dad and me—a father alone with his firstborn. The moment I set foot in his room, Dad asked me, "Sugar, does everyone get to go to heaven?" My moment of truth had come. My dying father was asking me, the one who had grown up hating him, how to get to heaven. Nine years later, I can still remember my exact words: "No, Dad, they don't. Jesus Christ is the only way that anyone gets to heaven. You don't have to clean up to come to God; He will accept you just as you are."

As those words came out of my mouth, Jesus instantly became real to me for the first time in my life. He was no longer a concept or a character in a Sunday school story. At that moment, I knew that Jesus was the answer to all my questions—past, present, and future. I was telling Dad that he could put his trust in Jesus, and I suddenly knew that I could too. At 9:00 P.M. on October 30, 1991, the destiny of a father and his daughter changed forever. We were *both* new creatures with a new outlook and new hope.

At 9:00 P.M. on October 30, 1991, the destiny of a father and his daughter changed forever.

High levels of morphine were still causing Dad to hallucinate, but the demons, flames, smoke, slime, and bottomless pit were all gone. My two sisters spent the entire night with Dad—our new Dad. Watching a basketball game was Dad's favorite thing to do, and he excitedly watched one on the ceiling of his room. Only he could see it, but what a gift that was! He sang songs to my sisters as if they were little girls and told the nurses funny stories all night long. I only wish I had been there to see firsthand my transformed dad.

Then in the early hours of the morning on October 31, Dad slipped into a coma. When I heard the news, I responded in a way so unlike the old me—with the peaceful conviction that God had everything under control. Around six o'clock that evening, my youngest sister and I were with Dad, and I felt led to tell him that I loved him.

"I love you too," he said faintly.

By the end of the day, Dad had told his entire family that he loved them.

The last time my father spoke to me was the first time he ever told me that he loved me. When the timing is right, once is enough. Once will last you the rest of your life. All those years of hurt, rejection, anger—and yes, even hatred—were washed away as if they had never happened.

A nurse called at 2:00 A.M. the next morning, November 1, to tell us that Dad was going quickly. My husband and I rushed to the hospital, but by the time we arrived, Dad had already gone on to be with Jesus. His hand was still warm to the touch, and I held it for the longest time, thanking God for all His miraculous blessings in the past four days.

To think that God would bring a new pastor to tell a dying man seeing demons about the love of Jesus. To think that Dad's life and my own would radically change forever—together and because of each other. To think this way seems impossible, but with God all things are possible.

Most importantly, God restored my trust. Only He could heal my old, deep wounds and replace them with beautiful memories. When I think of the angels who brought me back as I reached my arms up to heaven as a little girl, I truly believe that part of my purpose for staying on earth was to tell my father how he could get to heaven and, in the process, come to know that truth for myself.

I put my trust in Jesus, and He did for me what I never could have done for myself—He freed me from my desperate need for control. Now I trust my husband to wear the pants in the family. It's deepened our love for each other, and we are both happier. And I don't just sit in the pews of our church anymore. Now God is real and alive to me.

And who was the person God used to make it possible for me to receive all those blessings?

Of all people, my dad.

L inda is a busy wife and public speaker. She has been married to the same wonderful man, Jim, for twenty-eight years. Having left the business world eight years ago, she now speaks and teaches women and teenagers at church and at various women's gospel groups. She's also a member of the Precious Life Center speaker's bureau in St. Louis, Missouri. Linda is at amazingracemin@juno.com.

15

SINS OF THE FATHERS

Brian Waite

I don't know who my grandfather was.
I am much more concerned to know what his grandson will be.
ABRAHAM LINCOLN

I come from a long line of smart men who made foolish choices. In the Waite family, the sins and weaknesses of the fathers were passed down to the third and fourth generations.

One of my forefathers was a general during the Revolutionary War. His military career made such an impact that a statue was erected in his memory in New Hampshire. While this would be a source of pride for most families, we hang our heads in shame. One night, General Waite became so overwhelmed with fear at the prospect of battle that he abandoned his troops. Disoriented in the dark, he lost his way and rode around in a circle for hours. In the morning, his soldiers found him frozen in the saddle. The monument in New Hampshire commemorates not his superior leadership qualities, but his fear and foolish choice.

Near the turn of the twentieth century, Pearl Waite, a young steelworker who fancied himself an inventor, stumbled upon an edible crystallized gelatin that conformed to whatever mold it was placed in. He knew that it did because he tested it in his own work helmet. Sure that he was on to something big, Pearl pedaled his discovery door-to-door, only to face rejection after rejection. After two years of frustration, he gave up and sold his patented substance to a neighbor for twenty-five dollars. Within five years, Jell-O was selling over $1,000,000 worth of gelatin *per week.* Because of his foolish choice, Pearl Waite died broke and destitute.

My grandfather, Burl Waite, carried on the family legacy. My grandmother, a godly saint of a woman, passed away suddenly in 1939. Out of fear and distress, Grandpa immediately remarried. His new wife was much younger than he was and had few of my grandmother's virtues. The marriage was a horrible family scandal.

My father was only seventeen at the time. Highly impression-able, he concluded that his father's reaction to crisis was proof that God did not exist, and he abandoned the faith of his youth. His subsequent search for something that would give meaning to his life resulted in hardships and heartaches—four marriages, children raised in the custody of the state, and financial ruin.

It is amazing what we learn from our fathers.

It is amazing what we learn from our fathers. When I was twelve, my dad took me to the Texas state fair. There we encountered two of the largest men I had ever met. They weren't in a sideshow; they were fellow fairgoers. They wore lime-green T-shirts that read "Jesus Worker," and they asked us a question that would haunt me for years:

"Do you know where you would go if you were to die tonight?"

I didn't have a clue. The best answer I could give was "Sparkman-Hillcrest," the funeral home down the street from where we lived. But to my great surprise, my dad immediately said, "Heaven!"

After the men left, Dad said, "That's how you get those fanatics to leave you alone." Dad thought he was protecting his young son from the "crazies" of the world.

Three years later, we moved to a small farm community in Texas. Little did we know that this move would radically transform our lives. I had grown rapidly, and at fifteen I was six feet seven. Playing basketball was the greatest source of significance in my life. The problem was that I felt significant only when we were winning.

One of my teammates was another newcomer to our town. Jeff Montgomery lived his life completely differently than anyone I had ever met. He was not driven by his circumstances. He seemed happy and at peace whether we were winning or not. He had bought into something greater than himself and his circumstances. I found him so intriguing that I was determined to find out what made him tick.

My opportunity came during the middle of basketball season when Jeff invited me to an after-game party at his church. At that time, I saw no correlation between his outlook on life and his connection with church. I believed, as my dad did, that church was nothing more than a man-made organization designed to perpetuate myths and comfort weak people. I agreed to go because there would be girls and food—an irresistible combination for any teenage boy.

However, I found something I wasn't prepared for: genuine people who believed in something greater than themselves and who really cared for one another. For the first time in my life, I heard about the God who wanted to know me in a real and personal way. I didn't readily accept these beliefs—I was a skeptic, just like my dad—but I began to read the Bible, think about what it said, and interact with Christians besides Jeff. After six months, I knew I had to decide whether *faith* was going to be a theory or reality for me.

My epiphany came when I suddenly had to face my own mortality. When I was sixteen years old, Sam Castle, a friend of the family and a surrogate father to me, died of cancer. Before he passed away, he spoke to me about his personal faith and how it sustained him, even at the point of death. The day Sam died it was clear to me that I had to follow Christ completely or not at all—no more riding the fence of indecision.

On the night of March 11, 1981, I met God. I prayed to receive Jesus Christ as my Lord and Savior. No one led me. Alone, I yielded my life to God in a brief prayer that went something like this: *Dear God, I don't know what all this salvation stuff means, but I know that I can't do it on my own. My life is Yours. Forgive me and use me! Amen.* The prayer was simple, but it was all I needed to say to have a life-changing experience with God.

I was so excited that I wanted my parents to have the same joy I had just found in Jesus. Without realizing what I was doing, I made a poor choice by threatening them with God's judgment instead of showing them His love. I will never forget one night at dinner when I told Mom and Dad that they were going to hell without Christ.

I told Mom and Dad that they were going to hell....

Dinner was immediately over. Needless to say, my parents were not thrilled with my new-found faith. They thought that I had become one of the fanatics Dad had tried to protect me from years before at the fair. In fact, they were so concerned about me that they even discussed having me "deprogrammed."

Despite my mistakes, I began to see that, just as the poor choices had negatively impacted generations of my family, wise choices had the opposite effect. When the chain of sin was broken, there were amazing, miraculous effects, not only on my life, but on the lives of my parents as well. I decided to break that chain.

Even though my family abhorred my beliefs, they noticed a change for the better in how I treated others. After I met God, I showed them more respect and adhered to a moral ethic much more conservative than theirs. As a result, over time I saw them change from being atheists ("there is no God") to being agnostics ("there may be a God, but we just can't be sure"). For my parents, the leap from the impossibility of something to its real possibility was enormous. The door of faith was opening.

After I left home, I remained in contact with my parents, although we were a bit estranged because of my new exuberance and even more so because of my new priorities after I decided to go into full-time Christian ministry. That was tough for them.

While in seminary, I met and married Kathy. In the years that followed we had two boys, who soon became the apple of my mother's eye. Out of the mouths of babes comes much wisdom, and the boys were often able to raise spiritual issues with my parents in ways we as adults couldn't. In their innocence they would ask my parents questions like "Don't you want to go to heaven when you die?" and "Why don't you go to church?"

After the Gulf War, I was recalled to active duty as a chaplain in the U.S. Navy and sent to Okinawa, Japan, with my family. We were stationed there for three years, but at least once a year, at significant expense, we returned home to share the boys with their grandparents. It was the greatest gift we could give them. I yearned to break the old family cycle of living defeated lives, and I believed that if my parents spent quality time with my wife and kids, they would come to have a relationship with Jesus and find purpose in their lives.

In 1996, I accepted the position as pastor of Southwest Baptist Church in DeSoto, Texas. In human terms, the move made no sense whatsoever. I would make less money than I had as a chaplain, and I would lose my military pension. When my father questioned me about the move, I told him that I truly believed we were supposed to make this move in order to be closer to them.

That was the turning point for my parents.

Within eighteen months, both of my parents received Jesus as their Lord and Savior, and I had the privilege of a lifetime when I got to baptize both of them, just six months before my mother's death. They had, indeed, become new people with hope and purpose. They had made a wise choice.

I now have a wonderful relationship with my father, and—at least in this branch of the Waite family—the sins of the fathers are no longer being passed on to future generations.

In January 2000, after receiving a Ph.D. in historical theology, Brian moved to Edmond, Oklahoma, to serve as senior pastor of Quail Springs Baptist Church. He has written two books, *God's Top Ten* and *Choices,* and serves on the adjunct faculty of Oklahoma Baptist University.

16

FOR BETTY OR FOR WORSE

Betty Blyler

More marriages might survive if the partners realized
that sometimes the better comes after the worse.
DOUG LARSON

D ressed in a street-length, lacy shirtwaist dress, I stood
next to my dad at the back of the rural central
Pennsylvania church of my childhood. At the age of seventeen, my carefree life was coming to an end. As the organist
played "Here Comes the Bride," I thought, *There goes my life.* If a
miracle didn't stop me from walking down that aisle by my dad's
side, I would be leaving my very happy childhood home and be
bound to a husband—for the rest of my life! What of the other
boys who were still calling for dates? I'd be married…married to a
twenty-year-old boy I had met on a local beach exactly thirteen
weeks earlier.

Paul had showered me with compliments, and I had enjoyed
his attention. But just days after we met he started to talk about
marriage, and six weeks later he proposed. I believed that he loved
me, but I didn't return his love. I don't think I even liked him very
much. Paul was…well, he was….

Paul was certainly different from other boys I had dated. He smoked, wore a T-shirt and blue jeans on a date, and drove a loud, streamlined, two-door, hardtop '56 Chevy. I hated it! The sound embarrassed me, especially when he "burned rubber" in our lane after a date.

Nevertheless, when Paul proposed, I said yes. I had always been a people pleaser, and I thought that it was my job to make everyone happy. I didn't want to hurt his feelings, so I took the engagement ring, thinking I would find a way out later. But, always one to enjoy a new adventure, I got caught up in the preparations for the wedding and appeared to be excited about the upcoming event. Now I felt like I was on a roller coaster and wanted to get off, but I didn't know how to make it stop. Not one of the eighty friends and relatives gathered in the church knew how I really felt.

I stood at the altar still wondering how I could stop the wedding. What was I doing?

Now it was too late. While the soloist sang "I Love You Truly," I stood at the altar still wondering how I could stop the wedding. What was I doing? I couldn't believe I was saying the words: *better, worse; richer, poorer; honor, obey.* The words were sticking in my throat.

That was it. The wedding was over, and the marriage began. After the wedding, we headed straight to Paul's parents' home, where we were going to live because we couldn't afford a home of our own.

Paul had been raised in a Christian home. His parents prayed for their children, taught them the things of the Lord, and took them to a Bible-teaching church. They accepted me and treated me as if I were their own child. They offered me advice, guidance, and unselfish, unconditional love.

But there had to be more!

As a child, I had hoped to become three things: a Sunday school teacher, a secretary, and a mother. Going to church was a lifelong habit, and I taught Sunday school and sang in the choir. After high school I got a job as a secretary, and I kept it after I got married a year later. My final hope was realized when I gave birth to a daughter, Renee, in 1962, less than one year after our wedding day.

After Renee was born, Paul and I got an apartment of our own. I hadn't missed a Sunday at my parents' church for seventeen years, and we continued to attend there. Paul willingly went with me. In fact, he made no demands on me and let me do anything I wanted. He even quit smoking and got rid of that awful car.

So why was I so miserable?

The bottom line was that nothing Paul did was ever good enough. I quickly learned that I could order him around and make him live around me. I worked days, and he worked the night shift at a factory, so we didn't have to see much of each other. Even though I didn't want him around, I resented being alone every evening and having to make all the decisions and do all the family things with our daughter.

I soon resented everything about Paul. I was convinced that my misery was all his fault. He could do nothing to make me happy. I didn't like it when he talked to me, and I didn't like it when he didn't. I was annoyed when he went with me to a place I wanted to go, but I didn't like when he wouldn't. I was upset when he was out working on his car, and I was angry when he sat in the house watching TV. I didn't like it when he tried to be affectionate, and I didn't like it when he paid no attention to me. I didn't approve of the way he handled his money. I started to embarrass him by saying disparaging things about him, and I flirted with other men in and out of his presence. I had become so selfish that it was impossible for him to do anything to make our marriage better.

By the second year of our marriage, I was a very angry person. Our home life was falling apart, and I couldn't pretend that everything was fine. Paul and I saw each other only on weekends. When we did, I rarely said a kind word to him. I put all my time and energy into raising Renee and working as a secretary, leaving none for my husband. I felt trapped, and I wanted so badly to be free.

Paul began to feel miserable too, and he avoided me whenever possible. He would go to automobile races or to a friend's home to drink, work on cars, or just drive around in the car by himself.

By the time I was twenty, I couldn't stand living with my husband any longer. Three weeks before Christmas, I filled a laundry basket with clothes and took my two-year-old daughter "home" to my parents. I had no real plan; I just assumed that I would stay with my parents until I could get a place of my own.

A few days later Paul called. He told me that he loved me and that he would do anything I asked if only I would come home. He asked me to at least come home for Christmas "for Renee's sake." I said that I'd come home for Christmas, but that I would leave again the first week of January. I decided to go back for Christmas partly out of pity for Paul and partly because it would make things easier for me. Renee would have some semblance of normality over the holidays, and it would be less stressful to look for a place after Christmas.

I got through the holidays. Then, on the day I was to start my search for a place to live, both of our cars broke down. Paul and I were able to get rides to work, but I couldn't go apartment hunting. Now I was really trapped!

When Sunday came, we still didn't have a car, so we were forced to either stay home or go to church with Paul's parents. I agreed to go, knowing that I could get a visitor's card to verify my attendance and thus not wreck the perfect record at my own church, which was very important to me.

It didn't go well. At Paul's family's church the pastor talked about sin in a way I had never heard before—as if I personally had sinned! I was so angry. He had his nerve. I decided to ignore both what he'd said and the Bible verses he'd quoted about sin.

Another week went by, and our cars were not yet repaired. I still had no way to look for an apartment, and the only way for us to go to church on Sunday was to go with Paul's parents again. I had no choice.

This time the preacher talked about Jesus Christ in a much more personal way than I had ever heard before. None of the Bible verses I had learned as a child had helped me understand what "receiving Jesus into your heart" meant. But the preacher also said that we were *all* sinners. It seemed that he knew how horribly I treated my husband and that he was pointing me out, sending me a personal warning from God. While I was listening, the weight of my sin was so great that I felt as though I couldn't breathe. Why did he keep talking about sin? It made me so miserable and guilty. Again, I didn't like or agree with his message.

However, that week I started to see myself for the hateful wife I had become. I remember sitting next to Paul in the backseat of his parents' car. To this day, I can visualize the place on the country road where I said to him, "I feel miserable. Do you suppose that's the way you are supposed to feel when you go to church?"

Paul said, "I feel that way too!" Finally, there was something we agreed on!

After the second week, for some reason I was drawn to that pastor's preaching. As uncomfortable as it was, it made me think. By the third Sunday, our cars were fixed, but we still went back to hear the preacher who made us feel miserable. And we continued to go. It was an emotional struggle week after week for eight months, but we never missed a Sunday.

Why am I putting myself through this? I would ask myself. For years, attending church had been so easy, with nothing spiritually churning in my heart. Now the conviction of my guilt was so strong that I had to be free of it. *But if I believe in Christ as my personal Savior, I have to stay married.* I felt trapped, as if coerced into a commitment from something on the inside. *What should I do?* I wanted God to take away my guilt so I could be happy, but I didn't want to stay married. Many nights I cried myself to sleep.

In the meantime, the pastor's wife, Carole, befriended me. We lived near each other, and our children enjoyed playing together, so she asked me to her home on evenings when our husbands were both working. We baked cookies and talked about raising our daughters. It was my first good friendship in a long time. While she was befriending me, she and her husband, Glen, were also praying for me. Paul's parents, I was to find out, were praying for me as well.

Eight months after Carole befriended me, Sunrise Church, one of four churches in Glen's charge, held a week of revival meetings. Carole invited me to go, and I attended nightly. She sat with me and talked to me as if I were the only person there. When Sunday night came, Paul decided to go too. As soon as Pastor Glen started speaking from the Bible, after four years of being miserable, I finally broke down. Right there in my seat, forgetting that anyone else was around, I told God that I believed Him and that I would take His Son, Jesus, as my Savior and obey His will for my life. I asked Him not only to forgive my sins and my hatefulness, but also to help me stay married.

Amazingly, the weight was gone. In its place was peace. I wept with happiness and joy. Suddenly, I felt arms around me and knew that it was Paul. Right then, he was renewing the commitment to God that he had made as a twelve-year-old boy. It was at that moment that I became a new person—and so did Paul.

Then I thought, *I have to talk to Paul about this and ask his forgiveness for how I have been acting.* It was a miracle. I told him that I would stay married to him because I knew that it was the right thing to do and that I would try to be nicer to him. His response was incredible: He not only forgave me, but he also accepted me, even though I couldn't tell him that I loved him.

Divine strength enabled me to stay. I didn't automatically begin to love Paul, but I certainly did appreciate his willingness to forgive me for the way I had treated him. He saw an immediate change in my attitude. We began to share our emotions, and I started to treat him with respect. God was transforming me into a loving wife.

As I fell more in love with Jesus, I fell in love with my husband as well. Today I am very much in love with Paul, and I truly see him as a gift that God has given me. It has been many years, and our love is still growing. Looking back, Paul says that he can't even remember now how awful I used to be, because for more than thirty years, he has seen only the love of Christ in me.

Some years ago Paul and I built a house near Sunrise Church. Once in a while we walk up the hill to the spot where our new life together began, just to thank the Lord for all His blessings. We talk about how much we would have missed if we hadn't stayed together. These walks remind me that I had to meet God to learn that Paul was the perfect husband for me and that staying "trapped" in my marriage was, in fact, living free.

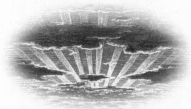

B etty has an M.S. in education and has been teaching in public schools for twenty-three years and speaking to church groups for thirty-five years. She is also the announcer on a monthly local program, "Time for Moms and Kids," on WMLP radio and the chairman and founder of Solid Ground Communication. Betty and her husband, Paul, are parents of two married daughters, Renee and Paula, and grandparents of three. E-mail: bdblyler@hotmail.com.

17

BACK IN THE GAME

Dave Dravecky

> *When God wants to do an impossible thing,*
> *He takes an impossible man and crushes him.*
> ALAN REDPATH

I grew up in a religious family, and I always tried to practice my family's faith. To me, that meant attending church once a week. Sunday morning was the time slot for respecting God.

But during the baseball season, going to church on Sunday wasn't easy, so when I was in the minor leagues, I went to baseball chapel—a brief, voluntary meeting held at the ballpark on Sunday before the game. I went so regularly that when I was sent to Buffalo, New York, I became the chapel leader.

We usually had guest speakers for chapel, and I heard a lot about God from them. But I didn't feel that I really needed God. I'd always depended on my own abilities, and I'd done pretty well with that. I thought of myself as a decent person. God still received His due on Sunday morning, but the rest of my life belonged to me.

I was playing for the Buffalo Bisons, the Pittsburg Pirates' double-A farm team. Double A is the midpoint in the minor leagues. Right above it is triple A, the top rung on the ladder to the major leagues.

Double A is definitely not a glamorous life. Very few of the players ever make the major leagues.

In the fall of 1979, after my first year at Buffalo, the Pirates, who "owned" me, asked me to play winter ball in Colombia, South America. I was not a bonus baby who had been signed for big money because I had a big future. In fact, I'd been told repeatedly that I'd never make it to the big leagues. So when they suggested I go to Colombia, I wasn't about to argue.

As a matter of fact, my wife, Janice, and I were excited about going. We had met in high school and gotten married right after college. We were two kids, married for one year, who had hardly been out of the Midwest. Now we were being sent to Barranquilla, a coastal city on the Caribbean. We had visions of tropical beaches and exotic Latin nights, which sounded considerably better than winter in Youngstown, Ohio.

We were totally unprepared for the Third World. Not only was poverty visible everywhere, but the weather was also unbearably sticky and hot. Right off, Janice got horribly sick. Most visitors from the United States got sick. We couldn't drink the water, and the food was barely edible.

During a night game, they would shut off electricity in half the city to get power to light the stadium. If you played poorly—and I did—people would throw corncobs at you. Fans figured out that Janice was my wife—she was the only blonde in the stands—and would hiss at her and make signs with their hands like a gun pointed at her head.

If you played poorly— and I did— people would throw corncobs at you.

It might sound funny, but it wasn't. We were miserable! We talked about God more than we ever had. But He was strictly a generic god, far from us, vague and unknown. We needed help, so out of desperation we both prayed. However, we weren't convinced that He could give us any.

I got sick with a 104-degree fever and was out of my head for days. Janice tried to keep cold compresses under my arms and on my legs while I thrashed around in delirium. She lay on top of me, trying to hold me down, praying that somehow God would help us.

I lost fifteen pounds in five days from the fever, and when I tried to pitch, I was so weak I had nothing on the ball. The team released me. When I got the news, I thought I was the luckiest guy in Colombia. The timing was great, just before Christmas. It seemed too good to be true: We would be home for the holidays. I promised Janice that we would *never* go back to Colombia.

The Pirates then sent me to play another year of double-A ball in Buffalo, and I had a good year—thirteen wins and seven losses. The key in the minor leagues is to keep moving upward. If you stay at one level too long, you'll be released. Too many other players are pushing upward, and they want your slot. That season I hoped to advance to triple-A ball.

But once again, the Pirates "suggested" that I play winter ball in Colombia, and I felt that I had no choice if I hoped to reach the major leagues. It was either go or forget about my future in baseball. So I broke my promise to Janice. She was really upset. She saw my point of view, but the memory of Colombia was too much for her. She couldn't stand it again. So we decided that she should stay home and wait for me.

I went back to Barranquilla—to the same apartment, in fact—without her. If anything, it was worse. That winter Jan and I had been married for two years, and I missed her like crazy. There were nights I got down on my knees to beg God for help because I felt so scared and alone.

With Janice so far away, the only companions I had were a few of the Christian players who would get together for fellowship. I'd sit in with them, not from any conviction that I belonged, but just because I was lonely. I listened to a lot of conversations about God. I certainly didn't buy it all, but I didn't reject it either. I guess I considered it like a college bull session where guys trade opinions.

It was no surprise that I pitched terribly and got released again. But this time I came home from Colombia a different person in subtle ways. I was no longer so sure of my ability to make life work in my favor. I'd learned that many things were beyond my control. I'd called out to God for help with more hope that He actually cared, which suggested that—though I couldn't have put this in words—perhaps He deserved more respect than one hour a week. My attitude toward Him was ripe for change.

After I left Colombia, I joined Janice in Sarasota, where the Pirates held spring training. I felt that I'd reached the do-or-die stage of my baseball career. I *had* to make the jump to triple A. It was play me at triple A, trade me, or release me. I thought the chances were pretty good that I would be released. That would definitely be the end of my baseball career—not something I liked to think about.

That spring, I sat with a bunch of guys talking about which ball club would be the best to play for. The consensus was that the San Diego Padres would be ideal because they had a great organization, the future of the team looked bright, and San Diego was a wonderful city. Also, the Padres' triple-A team was in Hawaii. Even if you didn't make it to the big leagues, you'd get to play in Hawaii.

A few days later, as spring training was winding up, Murray Cook called me into the clubhouse. When the farm director calls your name at that time of year, your heart starts thumping. All the guys were diving into their lockers, laughing, and pretending to hide from Cook. They began yelling, "You're out of here, Dravecky! You're gone!"

Murray looked at me and said, "We've traded you, Dave." Given the situation, that wasn't bad news. In the back of my mind, I was thinking, *Gosh, I hope he says San Diego.* Sure enough, he did! Immediately I was thinking, *Say Hawaii, please say Hawaii!* Instead he said, "We've traded you to San Diego, and you're going to Amarillo."

Where on earth was Amarillo? I knew for sure it wasn't in Hawaii. When I talked to the other guys, they said that Amarillo, Texas, was the worst possible place to play: hot, windy, flat, and dull. One of my buddies said that if he were given the choice of playing in Amarillo or hell, he would choose hell. Amarillo was a double-A team, too. It would be my third year at that level. *Oh well,* I thought, *at least I'm with a new club, and I have a new chance to prove myself.* I went to Amarillo, leaving Janice behind to earn money for us to live on during the coming year.

> *Where on earth was Amarillo? I knew for sure it wasn't in Hawaii.*

In Amarillo I checked into the Holiday Inn, where all the players stayed until we found other accommodations. My roommate had already arrived and was waiting to meet me. His name was Byron Ballard. I liked the guy immediately. Everybody did. He seemed incredibly joyful about life, and he had a wonderful, zany sense of humor.

Lying on his bed was some Christian literature associated with baseball chapel. I commented on it, and he asked me whether I was familiar with it. "I sure am," I said. "I was chapel leader in Buffalo." I saw Byron's eyes light up. He immediately assumed I was a "born-again Christian" and made a reference to that. I realized that I needed to straighten him out. "I'm sorry," I said, "but there's no way. I really don't understand that terminology at all."

Some people would have been rebuffed, but not Byron. He kept talking to me about God. Then he got out a Bible and showed me where Jesus talked about being born again as an Old Testament Jewish tradition. I was impressed. The guy obviously knew something I didn't.

During the following weeks, we talked again, and again, and again. Because of my experience in Colombia, I was open to rethinking my life. But Byron never rammed anything down my throat. On the contrary, I asked him questions. He didn't give me his answers to my questions; he showed me the answers in the Bible. For me that was very important because I had no doubt that the Bible was true. I already knew that there was a God, I considered myself a Christian, and I believed that the Bible was God's Word. But I had never read the Bible. Byron said to me, "Dave, I challenge you to read the Scriptures. I challenge you to find out who Jesus is and what He has done for you."

As I read the Bible with Byron, I got a new perspective of God that turned my religious ideas upside down. God wasn't distant and vague; He was active and close to people. God had come to earth as Jesus, who was visible, personal, and concerned about people like me—who, in fact, had died for people like me.

But I still had questions. I felt that I was basically a good person, so I had difficulty understanding why Byron thought I was a sinner. I knew I wasn't perfect, but did that make me a sinner? Byron showed me where the Bible says that all human beings are sinners because we all fall short of the glory God intended for us. We're not perfect. Why had no one told me this before?

I didn't become a believer overnight. I watched Byron like a hawk. It wasn't even what he said that convinced me so much as the way he lived. In every situation he was always the same: full of joy and brimming over with love for God. That's what drew me.

I kept calling Janice and pumping her with the stuff I was learning. She was horrified. She thought I was getting hooked into some cult. She said, "All I ask is that you don't do anything until I get there."

Colombia had shown me that I truly needed God, but it had had the opposite effect on Janice. It had made her doubt that God even existed. She had grown up believing in a god who was benignly taking care of the world, like a white-haired grandfather. That didn't square with the hunger, poverty, and hopelessness she had seen in Colombia, so she had concluded that there must not be any grandfather-god at all.

Although I hadn't known it, Janice had been deeply depressed—her simple, happy view of the world had been blown to bits. When she came to Amarillo, she was really nervous. She was afraid I was becoming a religious fanatic. We weren't communicating very well then. The last thing she wanted to hear about was God, and that was all I wanted to talk about. I wasn't very patient with her; I wanted her to see things the way I did and to move ahead as fast as I was moving. But we did love each other, and with the help of other people and a few books, she began sorting through her questions while I tried to be more patient. I saw her gradually growing as excited as I was.

Eventually, one blistering Texas day, Janice and I made a decision. We both committed ourselves to follow the personal God we had learned about in the Bible—to follow Jesus wherever He might lead us. We admitted to Him that we needed to be forgiven and promised to live our lives in His love from that time on, with His help. We met God together that day in Amarillo, and immediately life seemed to take a positive turn.

The next year, 1982, I finally made the big jump to a triple-A team. And I was sent to Hawaii! This time Janice came with me. By then, she was in the last six weeks of her first pregnancy. Two days after our daughter was born, I got a phone call to go to the big leagues. It was an incredible week for us.

In 1983, I was a new Christian, a new parent, and part of an all-star game. In 1984, I played in the World Series. In 1987, I was traded from a last-place team to a first-place team, the San Francisco Giants. That September and October, I pitched the two best games of my entire career. I threw a two-hit shutout to beat the St. Louis Cardinals. A couple of days later, I pitched an even better game. At the end of the year, I was riding high and thinking that 1988 was going to be Dave Dravecky's year. My plan was to win twenty games in the upcoming season.

But it wasn't meant to be. In October of 1988, surgeons removed a cancerous tumor from my left arm—my pitching arm—along with 50 percent of my deltoid muscle. "Outside of a miracle," the doctor said, "you will never pitch again."

"Outside of a miracle," the doctor said, "you will never pitch again."

But on August 10, 1989, I went back to the mound and threw ninety-one pitches. Before my surgery, I had thrown at eighty-eight to ninety miles an hour. In this game, with half of my deltoid muscle and 95 percent use of it gone, I was clocked at eighty-eight to ninety miles an hour. I don't care what anybody says—it *was* a miracle!

That game was probably the most memorable moment of my life, and I was so excited about the miracle of my comeback that I couldn't stop talking about it. My teammates were ready to stuff my mouth with anything to shut me up. My friend Bob just looked at me and said, "Dave, I hate to burst your bubble, but you know it's not the miracle of the comeback that's so important. It's the miracle of your salvation in 1981. That's the real miracle."

I didn't consider Bob a prophet, but what he said was indeed prophetic. Five hours later, I was on the mound pitching one of the best games of my life. Then in the sixth inning, I threw a fastball and my left arm snapped. I ended up on the ground with a broken arm. I was out. As they wheeled me off the field, I couldn't help but think about what Bob had said: The miracle of my salvation was what was important, not pitching a great game.

Cancer treatment had weakened my arm, and throwing fastballs put additional strain on it, causing it to break. This time my baseball career really was over. Eventually, my left arm and shoulder had to be amputated to stop the spread of the cancer. The loss was devastating. Janice and I both went through periods of deep depression, all in the glaring light of national media. But the lesson we had learned in Amarillo—that God is personal—had changed our lives forever. It kept us from giving in to bitterness and despair. Life isn't always fair, at least in the short run, but the Bible had taught us not to confuse life with God.

The most important thing I learned was that God had used baseball to give me a platform to give hope to others going through similar struggles. It wasn't the team I was on or how well I played, but being forced to quit and start again that gave me the compassion, understanding, and sensitivity I needed for God to use me for greater things than just being a baseball player.

Now I know that I am more successful than ever in God's eyes. Even though I lost an arm, I am now a more complete, joyful, and fulfilled person because I have found what's most important in life. I'm back in the game—the real game—and I wouldn't change a thing!

In 1991, Dave and Jan founded the Outreach of Hope national cancer and amputee ministry, which offers comfort, encouragement, and hope to those who suffer from cancer or amputation. They are also the bestselling authors of eight inspirational books, including *The Encouragement Bible,* and they publish a national newsletter, *The Encourager.* For more information contact Outreach of Hope at (719) 481-3528 or visit their web site at www.outreachofhope.org.

18

ALL THAT GLITTERS
IS NOT GOLD

Lori Trice

*A gem is not polished without rubbing,
nor a man perfected without trials.*
CHINESE PROVERB

I grew up in a charming three-bedroom, two-bath home on ten acres in the country. Outside in our beautiful garden, Dad pruned his prized wisteria trees, and Mom fussed over flowerbeds full of Shasta daisies. Inside, Mom made our home warm and inviting. My sister and I felt like princesses in the room we shared, with its canopy beds and matching bedspreads. My favorite room, though, was the kitchen, with its lavender flower wallpaper and matching curtains. Dad kept our garage perfectly organized, and I loved to sit and watch him work with his power tools. I can still smell the fresh-cut wood from the table saw.

My parents were popular. We went on picnics, threw neighborhood parties, and played family card games with friends. My parents attended PTA meetings, Dad took me to my school's Father-Daughter Banquet, and they both often helped friends with projects like wallpapering or building a fence. Friends and neighbors thought that my sister and I were lucky to be the children of such fun-loving parents.

Ours was a storybook home, and our family seemed picture perfect. But, as the saying goes, "All that glitters is not gold."

Despite how things looked from the outside, my parents had a loveless marriage. I don't remember them ever speaking pleasantly to each other. In fact, as I think back on those years before I was twelve, I can't recall them ever speaking to each other in public. Even at a card table, they always addressed other people cheerfully but never interacted with each other.

My parents were also totally unpredictable. When I got off of the school bus and walked into the house, I never knew what was going to happen. One typical evening remains in my memory.

The disposal ground up any hope that we would enjoy a pleasant dinner.

Mom had brought home my favorite dinner from Kentucky Fried Chicken. As we sat around the dinner table in our comfortable cushioned chairs, I eagerly waited for her to dish up our plates.

My anticipation turned to agony when Dad saw the three-bean salad on his plate. "Why did you buy this s——?" he snapped at Mom, shoving his plate to the center of the table. Mom replied that she thought he liked it. The argument escalated from there until Mom yelled, "Just throw it away if you don't like it!" Dad stormed over to the garbage disposal and threw it down the sink. The disposal ground up any hope that we would enjoy a pleasant dinner.

I know that my parents must have had violent fights when my sister and I went to bed. Many times we'd awake to shattered windows, damaged walls, and broken furniture. Occasionally, Mom had cuts and bruises. I don't know at what age I tuned out the sound of their fights, but I do know that for as long as I can remember, at night I had a loud box fan blowing at the foot of my bed, even though we had central air-conditioning.

My parents separated frequently, and when they did, we stayed with my mom's folks. I loved it there. The unpredictability of my life at home had made me fragile and insecure, and Mamaw and Papaw's home was a refuge for me. Mamaw worked at a bakery and always had lots of fresh-baked cookies, cakes, and sweet rolls in her kitchen. When I spent the night at their house, I often slept close beside my Papaw, wrapped up in his strong arms under a handmade quilt.

I remember Mamaw telling me that one night when Mom, my sister, and I were sleeping, Dad came over crying hysterically and pleaded with Papaw to go with him to our home, which was about ten minutes away. Dad had blood on his hands and shirt.

"You've got to come with me," he begged. "I've done something to Marie and the girls."

"Gene," Papaw said, "Marie and the girls are here, sleeping. You haven't done anything to them."

Unable to console Dad, Papaw went with him to the house to prove that everything was okay. But what they found was massive destruction. Every piece of glass in the kitchen had been broken. When Dad snapped out of it, he couldn't believe what he had done.

Eventually we moved back home, and Mom and Dad tried again, only to separate for good when I was twelve. This time Mom told my eleven-year-old sister and me that she and Daddy were getting a divorce, and we moved back to my grandparents' home.

Shortly thereafter Dad called Mom and told her that he had set our house on fire. Mom didn't know if she should believe him, but just in case, she called Joy, one of her best friends, who happened to live close by. Joy was pregnant with her third child at the time. She joined Mom, my sister, and me, and we went to see if Dad's threats were true.

The short drive to our house seemed like an eternity. When we arrived, the house was in flames, and we rushed to a neighbor's to call the fire department. As we were returning to my grandparents' house, we met Daddy on the road. What looked like a shotgun was sticking out of the window on the driver's side of the car.

Daddy ran us off the road, our car came to an abrupt stop, and a shotgun blast shattered both of our side windows.

Then things happened in a flash. Daddy ran us off the road, our car came to an abrupt stop, and a shotgun blast shattered both of our side windows. Joy died instantly. My sister jumped out of the backseat and crouched on the ground between the car and the ditch. Just then, Daddy pulled over and leaned inside the car. Mom was slumped over, apparently unconscious. I was stuck in the backseat of the car.

"Daddy, please, what are you doing?" I cried out to him. "Why are you doing this?"

"I have to do this. I have to," he said, more to himself than to me. He reached inside his car and pulled out a handgun. Then he put the gun under my mom's chin and pulled the trigger.

An instant later he seemed to return to reality. He looked at the destruction around him. "Oh, my God!" he cried. Then he put the gun to his head and shot himself.

Almost immediately, I heard the sirens. In a panic, I wrestled past the bodies of my mother and her friend, stumbled over the body of my daddy, and ran hysterically down the road toward the approaching fire truck.

The next thing I remember is sitting in the police car with my arms around my sister telling her I loved her. I asked the police officer to call my grandmother. I knew that she would come and get us and make everything all right, just like she always did. But almost as soon as that thought crossed my mind, I heard the police dispatcher say, "The grandmother has been shot."

Just before we met Daddy on the road, he had gone to town to kill Mamaw. After he had shot at her several times, Mamaw slumped over on the floor pretending to be dead. Convinced that she was dead, he finally left.

Mamaw spent several weeks in intensive care. She lost the eyesight in one eye, but, miraculously, she survived. She and Papaw began the overwhelming task of raising two emotionally traumatized granddaughters.

How did I survive such a life-shattering tragedy?

For as long as I could remember, I had thought about creation. I would gaze out at the stars at night and think about how wonderful God must be to have created such beauty. One summer four years before my dad drove down that road to destroy our world, our teenage baby-sitter had sent us to Vacation Bible School at a local church to get us out of her hair for a while. When the preacher spoke to that room full of children, it seemed as if he were speaking only to me.

He said that Jesus loved me and wanted to forgive all my sins. He explained that sin means doing things we know are wrong. Well, I had done plenty of that in my eight years. The preacher explained that those things separated me from a perfect God who loved me so much that He wanted to be close to me and walk through everything with me, protecting me along the way. I knew I wanted to have Him in my life. I talked to God right then in that crowded room. I prayed and gave my life to Jesus. That was the day I met God—the one who had created the stars and the moon I said good-night to each night.

That decision is what carried me through my devastating childhood. Even at the moment of my parents' tragic deaths, Jesus was right beside me. And His protection did not stop there. Jesus said that He would never leave me nor forsake me, and I have found that to be true at every stage of my life since that day at Vacation Bible School.

Over the past twenty years, God has granted me my childhood

dream of a happy home—on the outside and on the inside. He has blessed me with a wonderful husband and three children. By the grace of God, my children will never have to know what it's like to grow up in a tragically violent home. All that glitters may not be gold, but with Jesus my life has become a precious gem.

L ori is a wife, mother, Bible teacher, speaker, author, and singer. She is the owner/publisher of *The Community Church Guide,* a local Christian publication with circulation in the New Orleans area, and the coauthor of *Ordinary Women, Extraordinary Circumstances.* Lori lives in Kenner, Louisiana, with her husband, Brent, the pastor of River Fellowship Church, and their three children. You can contact her at loritrice@yahoo.com, www.riverfellowship.org, or (504) 466-0100.

19

NEVER THE SAME

Dr. Anna Rich

A half-truth is a whole lie.
YIDDISH PROVERB

This may sound strange, but I have known God all my life. But although I started calling myself "a child of God" when I was three years old, I didn't meet God personally until I was twenty-eight.

One night in 1969, I was watching Billy Graham on TV. Near the end of the program, Dr. Graham looked into the camera as if he were looking straight at me and said, "As the people are coming down from the bleachers in this stadium to receive Jesus, you in your living room...you kneel down and do the same!" All of a sudden I knew I had to do it. I got down on my knees right there in my tiny living room and asked Jesus to take over my life.

What happened next was quite surprising. We had just sold our home and were living in an apartment until escrow closed on our new house. When we had applied at the apartment complex, the manager had made it very clear that there were to be no more than two children per family unit. We had three. Out of desperation, I had signed the papers and sort of "hidden" one of our children—the quiet one!

I had rationalized my decision to sneak our third child into the apartment: *What would it hurt for a few weeks? After all, we're desperate, and we have wonderful children. The manager never questioned my answer, so see...God is helping us!*

But now I was saved! My first thought as I got off my knees was that I had to do something about the lie I had told. So the next morning, I marched with my three kids into the business office and told the manager that I was very sorry that I had been dishonest. I explained that I had seen Billy Graham on TV the night before and had asked Jesus in my heart, so I *had* to come and tell him the truth.

Much to my surprise, he allowed us to stay. I was so amazed that I decided that from then on, I was going to do things God's way and not my way. I wasn't going to just read the Bible, tell the stories to my kids, and go to church; I was going to put God in the middle of all my decisions and live day to day as a partner with Him. From that moment on, my thoughts, desires, and goals all became clear—and some of them have surprised even me.

In 1978, I started attending Bible college, and I now have four degrees, three of them in theology. Today I pastor a church, something I would never have dreamed I would do. This lady preacher remembers that night in April of 1969 when Billy Graham made the invitation, and is she ever thankful that she knelt down that evening and asked Him in! I've never been the same since.

Dr. Anna pastors a rural church in Fort Mojave, Arizona. She is a published author and poet and gives seminars on social issues from a biblical perspective. She has been married to Robert for thirty-six years and has one surviving child, Jim, who is a preacher and a businessman. Dr. Anna's e-mail address is Drannette@ctaz.com.

20

A RESTORED WORK OF ART

Jonathan Hunter

For those who believe in Christ,
there is no sorrow that is not mixed with hope—no despair.
There is only…a constantly going from darkness to light.
VINCENT VAN GOGH

Recalling the formative years of my life brings back a flood of memories awash with the loneliness that pervaded our home. My father, mother, and brother were present physically, at least for a short time, but because they were not available emotionally, our family had no cohesion. For different reasons, we were all very lonely at heart.

My father's alcoholism was obvious early on. By the time I was six or seven, I knew that he was out of control. Night after night into the early morning hours, my parents would argue loudly with each other. Unable to sleep, I vowed never to get married and have kids. I couldn't take the chance that I would be like my father and put them through what I experienced. I longed for a stable family life—but I feared it too.

My mother did her best to keep the family together and make up for my father's perpetual unemployment. It was clear, however, that she was not capable of taking up the slack; and in time, being the sole breadwinner took its toll on her health. At the age of

147

forty-six, when I was only seventeen, she resigned herself to the cancer that was ravaging her body. Having lost all hope, she also lost the will to hold on; she died, leaving behind two lost and lonely sons and a mere shell of a husband and father.

Because of a lack of bonding with my father, and yet a secure relationship with my emotionally conflicted mother, I felt very confused and insecure about my gender identity. In high school, I experimented sexually with girls—mimicking what the other guys were doing—but all the while, I was trying to quell growing homosexual feelings. They scared me.

After I graduated in 1967, I set off for a university in Florida— as different a place as I could think of from the staid Philadelphia suburbs where I had grown up. There, I thought, I could get a whole new start.

But in my freshman year, I developed my first male crush, which threw me into even greater confusion. By my second year, I was into "recreational drugs," and they became the means by which I abandoned my sexual inhibitions. In the summer of that year, I had my first real homosexual encounter with a friend while we were high on drugs. I swore him to secrecy—a promise he kept for only a few short weeks. Then the word was out.

After my sophomore year, I moved to New York to pursue acting. I soon got a job in a play that eventually toured overseas and led me to move to Paris to get into the film business. Two intense years of Paris, drugs, sexual chaos, and not much work brought me back to the States to try to further my career in Hollywood.

Los Angeles offered me lots of things, but stardom wasn't one of them. I immediately began using hard drugs and immersed myself in the gay lifestyle. It wasn't long before I bought into the prevailing idea that I must have been born gay, although I never felt comfortable with the label. And I always thought that the all-male social events I went to reeked of artificiality and narcissism. The prevailing attitude seemed to be: "We can't get acceptance in the heterosexual world, so let's create one of our own where we can do whatever we want."

The sexual idolatry in that environment was powerful and intimidating. In truth, I was as unfaithful as the next, always looking over someone's shoulder, hoping to spot that nonexistent perfect guy. Relationships, some lasting a month or less, some a year or more, always left me more dissatisfied and lonelier than before. I partied hard, sometimes staying up on drugs for two days at a time. The stardom I had pursued devolved into waiting on tables just to earn the money I needed to buy drugs for the weekend. I was desperately out of control.

That night, I had a very real near-death experience. I knew that I was dying and that I was on my way toward a terrible place.

Finally, on December 14, 1979, everything came crashing down when I accidentally overdosed. That night, I had a very real near-death experience. I knew that I was dying and that I was on my way toward a terrible place. Then Jesus came to me. I knew who He was, and I felt enveloped in His light. He told me that it wasn't my time yet and that now He was sending me back to finish what He had for me to do. That was the most wonderful experience of my life!

Days later, out of the hospital and feeling glad to be alive, I knew that I was beginning my life again. God had given me a second chance to live, and I was determined to find out who this God was that had rescued me from the precipice of death. What purpose could there be in bringing me back? I reached out to the only people I knew who would care.

My brother and his wife were Christians who were only too happy to embrace me and take me with them to church. Their obvious concern and compassion for my well-being—despite how I had raged against homophobic Christians—convinced me that there were Christians who really cared. They gave me a reason to keep pressing on.

On March 16, 1980, I was alone at a friend's house listening to a Christian tape that he had given me. On it, Hal Lindsay asked listeners whether they wanted to be left behind when Jesus came back, or if they wanted to join Him in the clouds. I felt that I had to make a decision. I remembered my near-death experience, and it reminded me that something profound was ahead.

The TV had been on mute, playing silently as I was listening to the tape, and I noticed that it was tuned to the Trinity Broadcast Network (TBN), a Christian station that I had never seen before. It caught my attention because it was a recast of a "Washington for Jesus" gathering. Thousands of Christians in Washington, D.C., were proclaiming their faith in God on the Washington Mall. As I saw the masses of people there taking a stand for Jesus, I thought, *I want to be with them. I want to be caught up with Jesus and join in the wonderful experience.*

I called the 1-800 number that was flashing on the screen, and the woman who answered asked me if I was ready to become a Christian. I said that I was, and right there I prayed to have Jesus come into my life. That night, over the phone, I met God.

I called my brother first thing and told him that I had just become a Christian. He told me that the previous year he had accepted Jesus into his life the exact same way—by watching a Christian television program for the first time.

Exactly a year to the day after my overdose, I was baptized in the Pacific Ocean. I was a new member of God's family, and I was changing.

The drugs that had consumed my life disappeared almost immediately after that phone call. Uppers, downers, LSD, cocaine, mescaline—all dropped off precipitously. I did cocaine once about six months after I met God, and it was a horrible experience that caused all of my old feelings and addictions to rise to the surface again. It was the last time I ever touched it. Within a year of my conversion, I tapered off smoking grass, the last of my former drug habits.

Leaving drugs behind wasn't difficult for me as a Christian, but dealing with my homosexuality was another thing altogether. Though I had read in my church bulletin about an ex-gay group called Desert Stream, I blew them off, thinking that they were probably just a bunch of pious losers.

Now acting and modeling more, I traveled a lot over the next few years. During that time, I had one six-month homosexual relationship, which ended in frustration. In 1981, I made the decision to remain abstinent to give myself time to get to know the new man in my life—Jesus Christ.

Within three years, two things happened that became catalysts for healing: receiving Colin Cook's tape series "Steps out of Homosexuality" and meeting the head of Desert Stream Ministries, Andy Comiskey. Through those tapes I came to understand that I was a heterosexual who struggled homosexually. Through my relationship with Andy, God brought me a mentor and friend who encouraged, guided, and challenged me to journey on to personal wholeness.

The drugs that had consumed my life disappeared almost immediately.

In the fall of 1984, I went through Desert Stream's "Living Waters" program for sexual and relational healing. Reveling in the newfound vision I had for gender wholeness, I was irrepressible when it came to sharing my discovery with gay friends. One of them ended up being the brother of a former partner of mine. He had AIDS.

Though I knew next to nothing about the disease, I was able to share with him my friendship with Jesus and introduce him to the hope I already knew. After months of prayer, just weeks before he died, he too received Jesus Christ as his Lord and Savior. Our shared experience convinced me that Jesus was the only antidote to the hopelessness surrounding people with AIDS.

In 1985, free and anonymous AIDS testing became available. I had been abstinent and healthy for four years, so when I went to get tested, I was sure that I was free from infection. However, I was still quite ignorant about how the virus worked. When the results came back HIV-positive, I was shocked. The consequences of my promiscuous past flattened me.

When the results came back HIV-positive, I was shocked.

Thankfully, Christian friends were there for me. Their unflagging faith and prayers continued to buoy me up and give me the lifeline I needed to stay emotionally afloat. The hopelessness of AIDS never had a chance to take hold for too long because of their steadfast spirit. My friends stood with me, holding me up, encouraging me, and demonstrating unconditional love for me by their presence. Only because of their love for God could they have loved me so much.

My faith continued to grow despite the grave prognosis for people with HIV. For years, a phrase ran through my mind over and over—*AIDS equals death; AIDS equals death*—like a tape on a loop. But just when I would start to slip into despair from the fear of death, God would pull me up, and I would begin again. He delivered me from ongoing spiritual and emotional circumstances that could have driven me to despair, and using either other people or truths from the Bible, He renewed my hope.

In the years since then, God has kept me healthy, allowing me to share my story in hundreds of churches, schools, and meetings all around the world. I always deliver the same message: God loves people with HIV and AIDS. To this day, I remain living proof that becoming HIV-positive is not a death sentence. However, only Jesus Christ can deliver us from the spiritual death and give us a truly abundant life. I'm living proof, for I now have that abundant life.

As C. S. Lewis once said, "We are not metaphorically but in very truth, a Divine work of art, something that God is making and therefore something with which He will not be satisfied until it has a certain character." The character, of course, is Christlikeness—becoming true image-bearers of God. I am one of His works of art, and, as my "author and finisher," He has placed me in a family that has the skill needed to restore me.

What a friend and family I found the day I met God!

Jonathan is currently the associate director of Desert Stream Ministries and author of the *Embracing Life* series. This series is offered through Desert Stream, an organization in Anaheim, California, that ministers to the sexually and relationally broken and to those with life-defining illnesses through healing groups and leadership training for the local church. For more information visit their web site: www.desertstream.org.

21

GOD'S DOOLIE

Jack Gilbert

Simplicity carried to an extreme becomes elegance.
JON FRANKLIN

My father was an Air Force general, and as a child I was determined to be a fighter pilot when I grew up. So when I was old enough, I applied to and was accepted at the United States Air Force Academy in Colorado. As a new cadet, I became a "doolie"—a term coined from a Greek word meaning *tool* or *slave*—and during the grueling summer of basic training, I figured out a cardinal rule for doolie survival: "Out of sight, out of mind."

After classes began in the fall, I got up daily at 5:30 A.M. to attend chapel services, but not for spiritual reasons. My roommate, Ron, and I went to chapel to avoid morning inspection, when our upper-class tormentors were the most irritable.

I succeeded in keeping under the radar until one Sunday evening in mid-September, when an upperclassman in our squadron paid Ron an unexpected visit. The cadet invited Ron to go to Colorado University the following Saturday with a group I'd never heard of—the Navigators. Ron declined because he didn't want to give up a Saturday he'd normally spend studying. I was dumbfounded. Only a fool would pass up a chance to get out of the all-male Academy for a day and meet some of Colorado University's lovely young women. So I turned to the upperclassman and asked if I could go in the idiot's place. There was a confused silence—doolies don't ask favors of upperclassmen—but then he shrugged and said, "Sure." So much for out of sight, out of mind.

Early the next Saturday, I boarded a dark blue Air Force bus for Boulder. Not really knowing anyone on board, I sat near the back, staring out the window hungrily at the expanses of freedom. Soon, one of the accompanying officers asked if he could sit down next to me. He introduced himself as Captain Jerry White, an instructor at the Academy and a faculty advisor for the Navigators.

The Navigators had started before World War II as a ministry to men in the military. They were active at the Academy and were going to Colorado University to do a survey on religious attitudes. Not surprisingly, the conversation quickly turned to spiritual things, and in no time Captain White had a Bible and a piece of paper on his lap and was showing me the Navigator's "bridge" diagram. After he drew a chasm, he put a holy God on one side, drew rebellious humanity on the other, and bridged the chasm with the cross of Christ. Then he asked me on which side of the chasm I thought I was.

While I was growing up, my spiritual experiences had been pretty much limited to Christmas, hit-or-miss visits to Sunday school, and the book *The Power of Positive Thinking,* which I read in high school. Although I read it to boost my self-confidence, it introduced the idea that God might just take a personal interest in me. But that day on the bus, I had no response—good or bad—and I noncommittally pointed to somewhere in the middle. Getting no further encouragement, Captain White excused himself and left me to gaze out the window.

When I got off the bus in front of the student center, I was paired up with a complete stranger—a tall, gangly junior cadet by the name of Ken Ake. We had a few minutes before starting out, so we sat down on a bench in a quiet hallway, and Ken asked me about my relationship with God. After about twenty seconds, I ran out of things to say, so I turned to him and asked him the same question. He swallowed hard, took a deep breath, and started in.

I remember his Adam's apple bobbing up and down nervously as he talked on and on.

It was clearly the first time he had tried to talk with anyone about his personal feelings for God, and he gave a long, rambling account of his spiritual journey. I remember his Adam's apple bobbing up and down nervously as he talked on and on, speaking more to the linoleum tile between his shoes than to me. But then he came to the part where he was standing out in a midwest cornfield asking Jesus to become the ruler of his life.

For some reason, at that moment a light went on in my head. Suddenly, the logic was irresistible. If someone wanted the very best, most satisfying life possible, how better to get that life than to entrust it to Christ? He knew and controlled the future, possessed unlimited resources, and had demonstrated by His death a far greater love for me than I had ever shown myself. I had absolutely no inner haggling or doubt as I waited patiently for Ken to finish his story.

Several minutes later, he looked up sheepishly and suggested that we get going. I told him that that was fine but that before we started, I'd like to give my life to Christ. His jaw dropped, almost hitting that linoleum tile he'd been talking to. "What...what did you say?" he stammered.

Unruffled, I repeated that I felt it was time to let Jesus be God of my life. When I asked him how I should do it, he stuttered that all I had to do was pray and ask. His suggestion was vague, but I took it and babbled some words. It didn't seem like anything had happened, so I suggested that he pray like he had out in that corn-field, and I would follow him. With some coaxing, he did. I did. And immediately I was filled with an intense mixture of gratitude and joy.

If I was pleased with myself, it was nothing compared to Ken's reaction. He dragged me around to the other cadets. His Adam's apple bobbed up and down, this time excitedly, as he asked me to tell them what I had just done. I calmly told them about my deci-sion.

I was totally unprepared for the congratulatory slaps on the back, whoops of joy, and even a few hugs.

With great enthusiasm, they actually had me memorize my first Bible verse to help confirm my decision. Thirty years after the day I met God, I still remember it: "God has given us eternal life, and this life is in his Son. He who has the Son has life; he who does not have the Son of God does not have life" (1 John 5:11–12).

Soon after, I woke up one morning and realized that my life-long desire to be a fighter pilot had disappeared. It never returned (well, maybe for a few seconds the first time I saw *Top Gun*). In its place, the desire gradually grew to help others discover the same profoundly simple truth that Captain White and nervous Ken, each in his own way, had communicated to me—that to God, we are never "out of sight, out of mind."

The love of sharing those life-changing truths led me into working with high school and college kids, then to seminary, and finally, much to my surprise, to Hollywood, where the potential for communicating truth has never been fully realized. For the past ten years, I've been working at Warner Brothers Studios, finding and training new writers for our television shows. This work has allowed me to communicate God's truths through both words and actions to the people I work with, and it has given me the opportunity to help elevate the character and craft of fellow Christians in the entertainment industry.

In a moment, years ago, I became convinced that entrusting my life to Jesus was the smartest thing I could possibly do. Thirty years have only confirmed the wisdom of that sudden, joyful conviction.

S ince landing in Hollywood fifteen years ago, Jack has been actively involved in both the professional and spiritual growth of hundreds of professionals working in the entertainment industry. Besides leading comedy and drama writing workshops at Warner Brothers Studios, he teaches regularly at his church and has organized rookie screenwriting classes, writing and creativity workshops, and groups to help writers discover the classics.

22

FAMILY MATTERS

Robert Hefner IV

*Happy families are all alike;
every unhappy family is unhappy in its own way.*
LEO TOLSTOY

S omewhere in the back of my mind, I was always searching for the reason for my endless discontent. Yet I was so preoccupied with preserving my family's legacy of financial success that it wasn't until I suffered a devastating loss that I found the answer.

I was raised in a very affluent oil family. It all began back with my great-grandfather, Robert A. Hefner. Great-Grandpa was one of seven siblings raised in a meager dugout home in Stephens County, Texas, where his family farmed the land. By the time he was twenty-one, he had been in school all of nine months. But he was ambitious, and through self-study, he prepared himself to become a lawyer. In 1902 he graduated near the top of his class from the University of Texas at Austin.

In 1901 a giant oil field known as Spindletop was discovered just outside of Beaumont, Texas. Seizing the opportunity, Great-Grandpa moved there to specialize in oil and gas law. Later he moved his practice to Ardmore, Oklahoma, where he won an important land case. His compensation was one-half interest in the lands he helped secure. Those lands turned out to be some of the most prolific oil- and gas-producing lands in Oklahoma, and they made Great-Grandpa a very rich man.

Shortly after he won the case, Robert A. Hefner was appointed to the Supreme Court of Oklahoma. After that, everybody called him Judge. By that time he had acquired thousands of acres of land and mineral rights in Oklahoma, Kansas, Texas, New Mexico, and Louisiana. Later, he served as mayor of Oklahoma City for eight years. The Judge lived to be ninety-seven, and I grew up in his shadow.

Robert A. Hefner got caught in the snare of the almighty dollar. Falling prey to the lure of money and power, his priorities became personal power, glory, and wealth. If anyone got hurt in the process…well, it was "just the cost of doing business." Since business success was his focus, his relationships were for selfish gain and his family merely an ornament. This pattern continued in the generations that followed.

My family worshiped and tried to emulate Judge Hefner. Robert Jr. was discouraged early on and gave up trying to succeed, but my father, Robert III, took on all of Judge's characteristics with fervor, and I tried to follow in my father's footsteps. My lessons started early in life.

Sometime before I finished first grade, my parents separated. Shortly afterward, my mother committed suicide. My dad was too busy being successful to deal with us children, so we were shuffled from nanny to nanny. With no mother and little relationship with my father, I was an insecure child. I didn't know where I belonged, who valued me, or whom I could trust. At an early age I built walls up around myself for protection. But I also watched and listened to see how I could gain the approval of my father and great-grandfather—approval I yearned for.

I was a close observer and a quick learner, and I mimicked my way to success. I learned that in order to succeed, I had to do it completely on my own. Though many people assumed otherwise, nothing was handed to a Hefner on a silver platter. We relied on our own will and skill. As a result, we all lived narcissistic, self-centered lives.

It goes without saying that a life at center stage does not promote unconditional love, trust, forgiveness, patience, and understanding. Like my father and great-grandfather, I focused on putting myself on top at the expense of everyone else—even my own family. In order for me to maintain the family name and the wealth behind it, my relationships automatically became vehicles through which I manipulated and exploited others for my own selfish purposes. I thought that in order to be great, I had to smash a lot of toes.

I thought that in order to be great, I had to smash a lot of toes.

I bought into this lifestyle hook, line, and sinker. After all, I was Robert Hefner IV, and I thought that everybody who was successful lived that way. I even believed that I would find acceptance, value, love, and happiness in such things as drugs, alcohol, and women. It seemed perfectly normal to me at the time. And besides, when I compared myself to people around me, I saw myself as better than the average person.

I did everything I could to feel satisfied and significant, yet in trying to "keep up," I was never content. Somewhere deep down inside I had the feeling that no amount of money would ever make me happy, but I didn't know how to process the thought because seeking money and power was all I knew. They were my weapons for survival and my ticket to significance. The truth was that I never felt valued because I had never experienced any real love or total trust from another person—and certainly not from anyone in my family.

I sensed a huge void in my life, but I didn't allow myself to think about it. Perhaps I was just too busy, or maybe I was afraid. Whatever the reason, I concentrated on working harder, making more money, gaining more prestige, and getting more power. Although I never spent much time trying to answer them, the questions were always there in the back of my mind: *What have I really accomplished? What does my life amount to? How much success is enough? Do I have any real significance? What do I really care about? What will I be remembered for? What do I want my tombstone to read?*

Then I met Carol. She had a Christian background and knew a lot about God. She seemed to have peace in her life—something I desperately lacked—and I was intrigued. As our relationship deepened, I experienced love and acceptance in a way I had never known. I didn't understand what made her life so different from mine, but whatever it was, I wanted it for myself. I no longer ignored those big questions in the back of my mind, and Carol encouraged my search for answers. Slowly, I drew away from the world of manipulation and deception in which I had grown up.

Marrying Carol was my first real commitment to anyone or anything besides my work and my financial dealings. Now I was asking what I wanted to pass down through my generations. What specific behaviors and values did I want to model? What did I want my new family to become that would be worth remembering? I wanted to establish new family traditions, new values, and new priorities. *But was that possible?* The closer I got to finding answers, the more I knew that I had to break away from the Hefner family ethic—a very scary prospect.

It took a devastating loss for me to give up the "security" of the Hefner family's wealth.

In 1993, our daughter Aliya was born with a rare heart-lung defect. For five straight months, Carol and I lived with her in the pediatric intensive care unit at Children's Hospital. Aliya survived multiple surgeries to correct the defect, and with each new day, we hoped to take her home. But just when we thought she would pull through, eight-month-old Aliya died in my arms. I was shattered. With her death, there was nowhere to turn for answers but to God. He got my full attention.

I had exhausted all my personal resources on medical expenses to save Aliya's life, and when she died, I had nothing left to my name. I was estranged from my family, struggling to start a new business in the oil and gas industry, and barely able to provide for my own family's basic needs. It was almost more than I could bear.

But in the midst of this life-shattering trauma, both at the hospital and afterwards, Christians seemed to appear out of nowhere. Friends, nurses, chaplains—even strangers— came to pray with us and comfort us. I kept asking myself, *Where have these Christians found this hope and peace? Who is this Jesus Christ who has brought them so much comfort?* Finally, I had asked the right questions.

Eight-month-old Aliya died in my arms. I was shattered.

I know that God allowed this terrible loss in my life in order to break down the final barriers that stood in the way of what I needed—a personal relationship with Him. When I look back now, I can see that all through my life, God had been preparing me to turn to Him—through people, circumstances, and things I read. He had been pursuing me all along, pushing me to ponder tough questions, reorganize my priorities, and make life-changing decisions.

Nine months after the death of my daughter, I finally surrendered. I gave control of my life to Jesus, and on May 15, 1994, I made a public confession of faith and was baptized at the same church where Carol and I had been married ten years earlier. On the day I met God, I was a broken man. After that, I was full of hope and purpose.

Because of my newfound joy in Jesus, I had an insatiable

appetite for the Bible. Its truths were illuminated for me as I poured myself into reading more about God and His unconditional love. The answers were laid out right there in front of me. No more searching. I was completely astonished when I read: "People who want to get rich fall into temptation…and into many foolish and harmful desires that plunge men into ruin and destruction" (1 Timothy 6:9) and "What good is it for a man to gain the whole world, and yet lose or forfeit his very self?" (Luke 9:25). These truths had been available to me all along, yet I had chosen to look the other way.

For the first time in my life, I felt an inner peace. All my insecurity and fears were gone, and I was able to break away from my negative family traditions and enjoy the peace that Carol had introduced me to years ago. I can now trust and love and have open and honest relationships. It's a new family tradition that Carol and I are passing on to our children and the generations to come.

R obert married the love of his life, Carol, seventeen years ago. They are the proud parents of five children, Robert V, Iman, Alexis, Aliya, and Gabrielle. Robert is active in his children's lives as well as in his church and community. He is now a geologist with the Chesapeake Energy Corporation.

23

Messiah in the Hallway

Mary Linderman

*Faith is like radar that sees through the fog—
the reality of things at a distance that the human eye cannot see.*
Corrie ten Boom

As a child, I was a good little Jewish girl with the world ahead of me. But as I got older, life didn't turn out the way I had imagined it would. I had a broken marriage and then an affair that completely broke my heart and brought me to my knees. At midlife, I was ready to give up. Life was too much for me, and I thought I couldn't go another day.

One night, I tried to end my life. I lived alone, and it seemed so easy to just down an entire bottle of pills, lie down on my bed, and drift off into nothingness. No hurts, no pain, no rejection— no more of that frightening hopelessness.

I grabbed for the bottle in the bathroom cabinet. As I did, it began to move away from me. I was stunned. I reached deeper and deeper into the cabinet, but the bottle stayed just out of reach of my outstretched fingers. Finally, I could reach no farther. In shock, I gave up. Once again, I had failed. I couldn't even end my life— let alone live it. Awestruck by the amazing phenomenon I had just witnessed, I abandoned my desperate attempt to kill myself.

Somewhere deep down inside, I suddenly realized that there was nowhere else to turn but to God. He was all there was now, so I started calling out to Him for help: *God, I know You're somewhere up there. I don't want anyone else, especially another man in my life. Just fill me up with You.* Little did I know then that God heard me cry out to Him from the very depths of my heart. I didn't know that He had already started to change me.

Weeks passed, and I continued to feel lonely, empty, and guilty. But this time it was a feeling that I had never had in human relationships. What was this? As my emotions intensified, days became more difficult and nights were endless. Once again I wanted to die, and I began trying to find a foolproof way to take my own life.

One afternoon, I was busy working at my desk at CBS when it suddenly seemed as though all sound had been turned off. It became deafeningly quiet. No phones, no TVs, no people—nothing. I quickly looked up. My office and all my surroundings had disappeared, and I was alone in another place and time.

My office and all my surroundings had disappeared, and I was alone in another place and time.

Then, from the distance, a solitary figure came into view, walking very slowly on a cobblestone street where the office carpet had been. His hair came down to His shoulders, and He was wearing a long white robe and had sandals on His feet. As He approached the doorway to my office, I saw His face—one I had never seen before—and I heard myself say, "Sweet Jesus." The words came from the mouth of a Jewess who had never even known anything about Him, let alone said His name—yet I knew that it could be no one else. He didn't stop; He just looked right at me and continued walking. When He was out of sight, the sounds, the office, even the carpet, returned as quickly as they had disappeared.

The wondrous ways of God—I had asked for more of Him, and He sent His beloved Son! That was the day I met God, and I have never been the same. After that clear, personal vision, God had free rein in my life. I not only began to learn about the Lord, but I also got to know Him personally and intimately—and what a revelation that has been! But most of all, I got hope. He gave me joy and eager anticipation of what each day would bring.

Since then, I've had my share of sorrow, struggles, and disappointments. Things still haven't turned out the way I once thought they would. But through it all, the Lord has been there, picking me up, dusting me off, and giving me His strength, His courage, and His great love to endure it all and go on. Through it all, that very vivid picture of Jesus, my Messiah, always touches my heart and brings me closer to Him. Now I am never really alone.

Until her retirement, Mary was an executive assistant in creative development at CBS television. She lives in Los Angeles with her dog, Coco, and enjoys spending her time with friends and her daughter, Marla.

24

THE BREAKING POINT

David Schall

*Only God can fill the god-shaped vacuum
that is within the heart of each of us.*
BLAISE PASCAL

A s a kid, I dreamed of being a politician, an actor, or a minister because all three careers commanded a stage and moved audiences.

When I was in third grade, I was our teacher's favorite student. Unfortunately, her daughter was also in our class. She was jealous of me and popular, so she and my other classmates began to call me a "sissy" and "teacher's pet." The taunts continued throughout grade school and junior high, severely undermining my confidence and threatening my self-esteem. I didn't resist their taunts, but I did find a way to fight back.

I was determined to prove to my childhood tormentors that I was a person of worth—a man of substance. In my resolute drive to prove myself, I not only acted in high school plays, but in college I also got into politics. I was elected president of my senior class, sat on the president's cabinet, and was named to *Who's Who in America's Colleges and Universities*. In my senior year, I ran the political campaign in Indiana County for the successful candidate for governor of Pennsylvania.

After graduation, I was offered a job in the new administration, and in very little time, I had worked my way to the top. I had a great deal of power and prestige, along with a sizeable income for a twenty-six-year-old. While I was working in the governor's and attorney general's offices, I even found time to act in several community theatres in central Pennsylvania. All the earthly signs of success were mine.

But somehow, it wasn't enough…something was missing. I remember walking in the park one night, along the Susquehanna River just two blocks in front of the looming capitol building. I looked up at the stars and asked, *God, is this all there is?* I felt unhappy and very unfulfilled.

On New Year's Eve 1975, I reached the peak of my restlessness and dissatisfaction with my career in government and politics. As the attorney general and I sat discussing the work of the justice department and his future political career, I thought, *I can't do this anymore.* He must have sensed what I was feeling because he suddenly asked me where I saw myself in five years. I took a deep breath and heard myself say that I wanted to be an actor. It was very hard for me to admit that, because I was his executive assistant and he was facing major political battles in the upcoming year.

He then said something that enabled me to make my decision. "David, Capitol Hill is filled with men and women who once had great dreams and aspirations for their lives. But because of fear, lack of discipline or education, early marriages, or having children when they were too young, they finally settled for a civil service or political job to pay the bills. And today, they are extremely unhappy and unfulfilled people. So, David, if you have a dream in your heart of being an actor and you don't pursue it, you will live the rest of your life not respecting yourself."

That was all I needed to hear. It took me eight months to get myself in a place to do it, but in September of 1976, I resigned from my government position, paid off my college loans, sold my car, moved into a New York Greenwich Village apartment, and enrolled in an acting school.

Once again, I was determined to prove myself. Since I had succeeded so quickly in government and politics, I assumed that I could easily make it in New York and that I would be a star on Broadway in no time. But a year and a half later, I was still not a star, and I was completely out of money. I had exhausted all my savings and my state retirement fund. I had been deeply rejected in a personal relationship, had made few friends, and had gotten nowhere as an actor. I had also been drinking myself to sleep with a bottle of cheap wine to dull my pain.

It's hopeless. I've had it. I'm totally lost and alone. I'm a failure. I give up! These phrases echoed through my mind on the cold winter evening of January 23, 1978, as I trudged up the stairs to my fourth-floor studio apartment. That night, I didn't buy the cheap wine, and tears welled up in my eyes as all my fears and feelings of hopelessness surfaced. I felt like an empty shell of my once confident, successful self. I hurriedly stuffed newspapers under my apartment door and threw blankets over the windows to muffle the sound of my wails. Unable to control my emotions any longer, I collapsed on my bed and cried until I could cry no more.

I hurriedly stuffed newspapers under my apartment door and threw blankets over the windows to muffle the sound of my wails.

Then in a quieter, more controlled desperation, I got down on my knees beside my bed. I had always thought that I knew God. After all, I had been baptized at birth and confirmed in my family's church at the age of twelve. I had even held positions of leadership in church youth groups. Yet God had never really been an intimate part of my life.

Now I prayed as I never had before. Humbling myself had never come easy to me, but this time it was my only option. I was ready to surrender all. Through a flood of tears, I admitted to God that I could no longer go it alone, that I was filled with fear, and that I needed His help. Though I hadn't been able to admit it before, my fragile ego had always been the center of my life. I asked Him to forgive my foolish, selfish pride and my sins. At that moment, intimate and serene, I surrendered—I invited God's Son, Jesus Christ, to come into my soul, my mind, my life, and take control of the mess I'd made.

Just as I finished praying that prayer, a deep peace flooded my mind and body. Suddenly the fears and anxiety, all of the emotional turmoil, completely ceased—totally gone in an instant! I knew then that I was experiencing what I remembered reading in the Bible about "the peace that passes all understanding." I knew that something profoundly important had taken place. God was real and was actively pursuing a relationship with me—me, who had ignored and taken Him for granted for so many years. That was the exact moment I met God.

I lay there on the floor of my apartment basking in that peace. It felt as if I were lying on a buoyant cloud, floating about the room in God's presence, completely sinless and pure in His eyes. I didn't want that feeling to end. Eventually, after what seemed to be two hours, I got up to blow my nose and wipe the tears from my face. I gathered up the newspapers from under my door and took the blankets off the windows.

Sitting on the edge of my bed, still enjoying my newfound peace, I realized that I'd never really consulted God before beginning my acting career. I didn't become fearful, but simply knelt again on the floor beside my bed, thanked God for coming into my life, and asked Him to show me whether it was His will for me to continue pursuing an acting career, go back to my government job, or serve Him somewhere else. This relationship with God was a new thing—two hours old, to be exact—and I really needed a specific sign, one that would show me beyond a doubt that it was from Him.

About an hour later, the telephone rang.

It was 11:30 P.M., so I assumed that it was a family member calling after the eleven o'clock rate change to save money. But the caller identified himself as the director of an industrial film that I, along with three hundred other candidates, had auditioned for that afternoon. He was calling to tell me that I'd been given the lead role in the film. It paid five hundred dollars a day! The only problem was that filming started the next day. He was apologetic about calling so late, but was I available? Was I interested? Was I interested!

The call couldn't have been more confirming. I accepted the job, thanked him, hung up, and got down on my knees for the third time. I thanked God for honoring my earnest prayer and giving me an unmistakable sign. I thanked Him for His direction and His reassurance that everything was going to be okay.

That was the beginning of a new life built on a new foundation. I continued acting, later moved to Los Angeles, and now, along with my acting career, I run a ministry for Christians in the entertainment industry, both in L.A. and New York City. My seemingly failed career grew into a fulfilling vocation that utilizes all of my political and performing skills. In fact, I've done everything I had wanted to do as a kid. I've been in politics, found satisfaction in acting, and am now focused on ministry.

More importantly, as I've grown in my relationship with God, I've learned that though He loves me unconditionally, He isn't necessarily interested in what I do professionally. He uses what I am passionate about to lead me closer to Him, and then I allow Him to work through me in my chosen profession. Although I had once been rejected because I was my teacher's favorite, I'm thankful that I have the favor of God. He wants me to grow where I am planted in my love for Him and to impact for eternity the lives of the people He has placed around me. God didn't call me to be successful. He called me to be faithful.

That night twenty-three years ago was the turning point in my life. Anxiety and rejection are still part of the scene. But now I have God's strength, hope, and wisdom to deal with them, and that makes all the difference.

David is co-founder of Actors Co-Op, a professional company of Christian actors in Los Angeles; founder and director of Inter-Mission, a thirty-eight-hundred-member organization; and founder of Act One: Writing for Hollywood. He also serves as the executive director of the Department of Entertainment Ministries at Hollywood Presbyterian Church.

25

JESUS ON THE FRIDGE

Bob Anderson

The affection of a father and a son are different:
The father loves the person of the son,
and the son loves the memory of his father.
ANONYMOUS

I was just beginning kindergarten when my mom told me that Dad was going to be living somewhere else—for the rest of our lives. My tiny kid brain was incapable of absorbing such a huge concept and quick to deny the reality of something that sounded so painful. But, as if totally unaffected, I chirped, "That's too bad. He's a nice guy." Then I ran off to play, trying to escape the words that Mom had just spoken to me.

I cried myself to sleep often while I was in elementary school. It just didn't make sense to have a dad and then to not have a dad, just because he wanted to live somewhere else. What had I done wrong? Why did he want to leave me? He did come to visit us at Christmas, but his visits were bittersweet. He was always nice to us—sweet—but after the presents were opened and dinner was over, he'd leave—bitter. Our relationship over the years was shallow at best.

As I grew older, my memories of Dad became fewer and more

faded. But there are some I have even to this day. The videotape of my mind has held onto a clip of him holding me in his strong arms. He was wearing a red Pendleton, very soft. In the second clip, we are both laughing. Dad had hidden behind some bamboo in a friend's backyard while we played hide-and-seek. He popped out of nowhere and startled me. We laughed. Then he chased me. Such an isolated moment, but frozen in time in the gallery of my heart.

I didn't let my dad's absence kill me. I fought back in the only way I could—by finding ways to achieve in life. I felt that if I excelled, my actions would state: "Even though my father left, I am worth something. Just look at this!" When I finished junior high, my drive to succeed reached a fever pitch.

High school was a very important time in my life. It was then that I became a photography freak. I was absolutely passionate about images. I soon discovered a creative ambition rising inside of me that drove me to work in the darkroom through many late nights. At sixteen, I was a workaholic!

I threw myself into photography because it gave me a new sense of mission and identity. I received many awards, even one from the former photo editor of *Look* magazine. The awards banquets and praise I enjoyed were especially gratifying, and for a short time they helped fill the huge black hole in my heart. It was as if a whole new vista had opened up to me. For the most part, instead of getting lost in drugs, partying, or racing my hot car on the boulevard, I was infatuated with the thrill of creating new images. I was having an absolute blast!

Not only was it rewarding to realize my talents, but my accomplishments also brought me the admiration of my peers. I developed a reputation as the top gun in my photography class. It felt great. But all the accolades in the world weren't enough to fill the void in my life. The thrill invoked by my new love of photography couldn't resolve that deeper conflict within me. As much fun as I was having walking down my path of glory, I often cried myself to sleep at night.

During the day, however, I loved my life. I loved all the neat things that were going on in school, and I especially loved my photography. I had neat friends. I had the best mom in the world, and I had a sister that I actually sort of liked. But mixed in with these fabulous feelings of youth—aptly epitomized by so many of the Beach Boys' songs of that day—there was a deep pit of utter lostness. Sure, my parents' divorce contributed to both my drive to succeed and my sense that something was missing in life, but the fearful reality settling into my soul was that my lost condition was far greater than anything I could control, imagine, or measure.

But mixed in with these fabulous feelings of youth, there was a deep pit of utter lostness.

At times when I was alone, I began to reflect back on a profound moment in my childhood. My neighbor, Mrs. Camara, had often baby-sat me. One day when I was four, while I was at her house galloping around on my stick pony, I suddenly noticed a portrait of Jesus on top of her refrigerator. I asked her who that man was, and she said, "Bobby, that's Jesus Christ, the Son of God." I said, "Oh," and resumed racing my horse around the house. But her words—"Jesus Christ, the Son of God"—had pierced my heart, and somehow I understood the significance of her reply. I believed what Mrs. Camara had said, and in times of crisis I often prayed as a kid, but as I grew older, I didn't have an ongoing interest in Him.

About the time I started thinking a lot about those powerful words from years ago, my two best friends in high school, who didn't know each other, both became Christians. Soon, each friend found his own opportunity to tell me about his newfound faith. But what did I do? I argued with them! Even though I believed that Jesus was a special leader of spiritual importance, I rejected the notion that He was the only way to salvation. "Salvation from what?" I asked. So I argued, and in both cases, I proudly felt that I had won the argument.

I fought diligently to keep Jesus Christ from entering my life. I truly did respect Him. No…more than that…I revered Him. But I didn't want Him controlling my life. One reason was that I didn't want to become like another one of my neighbors, "Mrs. M."

Even as a child I recognized the difference between Mrs. Camara and Mrs. M. Mrs. Camara, who kept Jesus on her fridge, had left a positive image in my mind. She loved God and was very gentle. Mrs. M., on the other hand, was a staunch member of a Christianlike cult. She was loud and pushy, acted superior, and had a strange veneer of pseudospiritual sweetness that turned my stomach. When my friends told me about their faith in Jesus, Mrs. M. and all of her baggage came to mind. She was what I didn't want to become.

I was also very stubborn. Hearing, even from my friends, that I had to believe in Jesus Christ in order to be forgiven of my sins made me recoil. I was eighteen. By then, I had tasted plenty of success, and my sense of independence was number one on my list of controlling interests. I feared having to give all that up for God. My attitude was: *This is my life; I'm doing fine with it; and Jesus can just stand at a safe distance, thank you very much.*

So when my two friends told me about their faith in Jesus, I set my heart in stone and cast aside their words, rejecting God in a definitive way for the first time in my life. And I got just what I chose: life on my own terms and a continued sense of being lost.

The results of my turning away from Jesus soon became evident—I became like Mrs. M. A friend of mine got me hooked into a cult that claimed that *all* roads lead to God, not just one. They even included Jesus as one of the many paths. I was proud of being "open-minded." I figured that if they said nice things about Jesus, however inaccurate or loony, this tolerant group of thinkers must be okay. I respected Jesus. I just didn't want Him as my Lord and Savior. So a friend and I joined the cult. We got mail-order lessons from a guru on how to meditate on our "third eye" and become one with the "cosmic Christ consciousness and the Divine Mother."

Then it happened. As I started meditating on *nothing*, I lost my ability to concentrate. Unpleasant and unnerving thoughts filled my mind. I meditated harder and longer, but things just got worse. Darkness overshadowed my entire life.

Soon, this mysterious oppression was attacking me full force every waking second. Hideous thoughts forced their way into my head. Profane words and ghastly images played like a tape loop in my mind. I thought I was going insane.

We got mail-order lessons from a guru on how to meditate on our "third eye" and become one with the "cosmic Christ consciousness and the Divine Mother."

After seven agonizing months of mental torture, I finally remembered what Mrs. Camara had said to me when I was four: "That's Jesus Christ, the Son of God." I remember the impression that name had left on my heart when she spoke those words. Then it hit me—they must be true! I got down on my knees and prayed a very unreligious prayer, something like, "Jesus...the one on the refrigerator, you know, at Mrs. Camara's...I'm here!" Next, I called one of my friends who had told me about Jesus in high school, and that Sunday I went to his church.

When we arrived, I was ushered into a room where the youth group met. Even before the class began, an outspoken kid with steely blue eyes and bright blond hair turned his head, looked me in the eye, and said, "Have you accepted Jesus Christ as your Lord and Savior?" I didn't even know the kid's name, but he wouldn't let up on me. Finally, that morning in this strange Sunday school class, I asked Jesus to take control of my life. From that point on, it was like the Lord lifted me up and at light speed put me on the road to an amazing adventure.

When I let go and let God have control of my life, He filled the void left by my earthly father's absence. My lifelong dream of a relationship with a loving father finally came true. He had been there all along, passionately waiting for me to call home. And of course, He has done far more than that. Where there once had been a spiritual vacuum the size of a black hole, there was now peace and fulfillment. When I stopped resisting and allowed Jesus to come into my life, I became a "new creation," not an alien life form. When I gave Him my life, I suddenly realized that Christ had transformed me into the person I had always longed to be.

Where there once had been a spiritual vacuum the size of a black hole, there was now peace and fulfillment.

And that's not all! As God melted my heart and healed the hurts of my past, I was able to reach out to my natural father. One day, after I had gotten to know him, I said, "Dad, I'm so impressed with you. I really am!" He was amazed that I was so affirming of him. It was more than he could take. He left the room shaking his head and saying, "I sure don't see why."

It broke my heart to see Dad's sense of self-worthlessness, but I just kept loving him. Years later, I was able to spend priceless time with him as he lay on his deathbed. I'll never forget the amazing, healing words he spoke to me in that hospital room. He looked me straight in the eye and said, "Bobby, you're the best thing that ever happened to me."

Divorce had broken my father, and in turn, his brokenness had torn my life apart. Then the heavenly Father entered my life and began healing me. As Jesus made me whole, I was able to reach out to my dad—the original source of much of my pain. Our lives came full circle when my dad turned his life over to Jesus during the final days of his life. He too was made whole, and now he's in heaven, laughing in the strong arms of his Father.

What a beautiful image of redemption—even better than the picture of Jesus on the fridge!

B ob was one of two key producer/directors at Harper Films in California for fifteen years. He has also worked as a video producer, cinematographer, writer, special effects designer, and editor. His work has won more than fifty national and international film awards, including an Emmy. You can reach Bob at client77@aol.com.

26

A Creature of the Dark in the Light of the Dawn

Ruth

A glimpse is not a vision.
But to a man on a mountain road by night,
a glimpse of the next three feet of road
may matter more than a vision of the horizon.
C. S. LEWIS

Why won't someone save me? Hiding in the closet never worked—I was afraid of it too. It was next to the rafters, and I was terribly afraid of falling through the beams. But my fear of being caught and punished was much worse. What I was being punished for never mattered. I curled up tightly in the dark under the hanging clothes and tried not to breathe or wet my pants. I heard the sound of footsteps and an angry voice calling my name. *If I just live through this, I will grow up and be safe,* I thought. The footsteps stopped, and light flooded my hiding place. No one was going to save me.

Blinding light always preceded the blows.

When I was three years old, four boys from outside our neighborhood molested me. I had sneaked out of the house when I was supposed to be taking a nap, and the boys enticed me to a garden shed out of sight of my house. Afterward, stained, I stood blinking in the sun, crying. My mother found me and dragged me home by the hand so fast that my feet hardly touched the ground.

"You're a bad girl!" she told me over and over. "This is all your fault."

Later that year a relative started to molest me during family visits. As I got older, he drugged and raped me. His mistress got involved in the abuse, which included occult practices. By then, I had learned to shut down during these incidents and block out my memory of them. *I was a bad girl,* I thought, *and it was all my fault.*

By the time I was seventeen, I was a confused, angry, headstrong girl who wanted to run as far as possible from everything I knew. I went into the military, volunteering to serve at a base in Europe to be near my grandmother, the only person I felt really loved me.

I was far away from the scenes of my past, and the freedom was exhilarating. Without censure, I sampled every pleasure I had read about during my lonely childhood. I was having such a good time!

I sampled every pleasure I had read about during my lonely childhood.

Never mind the bandages on my wrists; that was just a momentary low. If I could just get enough pleasure, I thought, surely it would make the horrendous ache in my chest go away. But it didn't.

I met Pete long before I was ready for marriage, but I married him quickly, afraid that he would go away and I would never again find someone who wanted to take care of me. I loved him as much as I was capable of at the time, but my behavior and thoughts were distorted from the years of sexual abuse. I carefully hid the truth from him because I knew he couldn't love the real me. No one could.

We had a son. Heavy internal scarring prevented a normal delivery, and he was born two months premature and very ill. My behavior changed enough to accommodate the baby's needs, but no real improvement came. I was sexually promiscuous whenever my husband was away—which was often. When I was honest with myself, I had to admit that I was miserable. I really did love my husband and child, but I felt powerless over the addictions and behaviors in my life. Life spiraled downward, and I knew my marriage would never last.

What a horrible creature I was! I didn't deserve to be happy.

I thought about my options. Suicide—going down in flames, living life in total self-indulgence to the point of death. Reform. Hah! How would I do that? As a teenager, I had flirted briefly with Christianity, but when the Christians I met proved human and frail, I felt judged. So I dropped it and ran. Now I thought about it again, but again I couldn't separate the people from their God. They'd never accept me.

Still, I did have one friend, Elaina, who truly seemed to accept and love me as I was, even though she was a Christian. During a business trip to Spain, I was bored, soul sick, and desperate for something to read. Elaina offered me a book on the Christian principles of marriage. The normal fare on military trips was pornography, which was passed around the hotel from couple to couple. I realized that I preferred the porn, and, suddenly ashamed, I took the book Elaina offered.

I was amazed at what I read. The book said that a happy marriage was possible, even for me. Not only could my marriage be saved, but I could as well. It was almost more than I could take in. I wanted it so badly! I read the prayer in the book asking for salvation through Christ, and immediately the assurance of my salvation and forgiveness for my past lifted me out of my pit.

That was the day I met God. Exhilarated, I literally danced to Elaina and picked her up in a bear hug. I told her that I had read the book and accepted the Lord. Amazed, she rejoiced with me—I was a new creature!

God began to change my darkness into day, one step at a time. Daylight can be a scary place for a creature used to the dark. Above all, I feared rejection. But I could tell that God had His arms around me. He continually showed me His gentleness and patience and let me know in hundreds of ways how much He loved me. He showed me how He was healing, changing, and directing me.

He brought loving Christians into my life to accept and mentor me. I found I was starving for that kind of unconditional love. My husband and I grew closer, and God gave us a daughter to bring us joy along the way. We had Bible studies, sang in the choir, and stayed active in the support groups and ministries around us.

Daylight can be a scary place for a creature used to the dark.

For ten years I walked in the light, and my relationship with the Lord flourished. Then a series of blows put my faith in the furnace. One day I was in a serious car accident, and it triggered severe emotional problems. I fell into a terrible depression that would not break. Then I was diagnosed with a tumor. At the age of thirty, I had a total hysterectomy and went through instant menopause. I suffered a severe bout of anorexia and got dangerously thin, losing much of my hair and loosening my teeth in the process.

As my depression deepened, I was suddenly bombarded with the memories I had buried as a child. The threats, abuse, drugging, and rape flooded my memory. My affairs escalated as I hysterically tried to get away from the pictures in my head. I was certain I was losing my mind. I suffered a total collapse and was admitted to a psychiatric hospital. During that long, horrible time, I was diagnosed with bipolar disorder, or manic depression.

Though I was frightened of the diagnosis, it seemed to make sense as I looked back over my life. Intellectually, I knew that God was there—I had the track record to prove it. But my fear made me *feel* completely alone. If God had abandoned me, I must have deserved it. Why would He save me? Why would anyone save me? Raw parts of me that had not seen the light of day in thirty years wanted nothing to do with a God who would let such horrible things happen to me.

Hypnotherapy sessions recreated every trauma as if I were there. I spent day after day curled up against the wall between my bed and desk, not talking or moving for hours at a time. Could I serve a God who allowed such pain? I reached the absolute end of myself then. Physically, emotionally, and mentally there was no more to draw upon. I didn't care if I ever left the hospital. I was just taking up space.

My God, my God, why have You forsaken me?

One day I was lying with my eyes closed, feeling adrift and cold, when I saw a "spark" in my mind's eye. It was inside of me, tiny, but bright and unwavering. I could feel warmth from it. Instantly I knew that it was God. The glow grew, and I felt love, acceptance, and protection wash over me. For the first time in my life, I really understood what Jesus had done for me. He had gone through hell and come back to serve. He was there to help me to begin again, right where I was and where I needed Him to meet me. At the time I needed simple imagery and feeling, and He gave me that light and warmth inside of me.

> *It was inside of me, tiny, but bright and unwavering. I could feel warmth from it.*

Over the next few days, God drew me back to the Bible to read His promises and encouragements. Over the next two weeks, He renewed my commitment to go home to my family.

This was a huge and scary thing. When I returned home, I felt alienated from normal people. My family was very patient and kind, hugging me often and letting me slowly adjust to the world. They were my cushion and hedge of protection. But I was afraid to tell them where I had been on my emotional and spiritual journey. My children were too young, and my husband had his hands full trying to deal with the aftermath.

At first I made the mistake of looking for Jesus "with skin on." Christian friends I knew and loved—but who didn't understand my illness or my past—insisted that I was sick because of "demonic attack" or not "claiming" healing from the Lord. "God cannot want you to live this way," they'd say. It caused both my family and me great frustration. But, over and over, God gently pulled my gaze away from them to Him. And when it really hurt, He was there, inside my broken heart, waiting for me to let Him quietly work. I didn't have to do anything; I just had to want Him.

That was a very tough hurdle to get over in my mind. I wanted the pain to go away as proof that He loved me—the same reason I had wanted it to stop as a child. When it finally dawned on me that Jesus would work through the pain, not in absence of it, I began to see a light at the end of the tunnel. It also enabled me to deal with those who thought that I should be instantly delivered from my pain and struggle.

That's what has enabled me to move on—knowing that coping with my past and present is a process, not a destination. I still have those feelings from the past, but I am learning to go on without acting on them because I know that they are not reliable indicators of where or who I am. As I live out this truth one day—sometimes one moment—at a time, God is healing me one wound at a time.

As a child, I had cried out for someone to save me from my pain. When no one did, I thought that it must be my fault and asked myself why anyone would want to save me. But someone did want to, and I am alive today because He did.

R uth and her husband, Pete, are screenwriters in Los Angeles, where they live with their two children and minister to professionals in the entertainment industry.

27

GOOD NEWS FOR A
THOROUGHLY MODERN MAN

Michael O. Sajbel

If we live good lives, the times are also good.
As we are, such are the times.
ST. AUGUSTINE

Within a few weeks of my birth, as is customary in the Catholic church, my parents had me baptized. That evening my mother excitedly called my grandfather in Iowa and proclaimed, "We just baptized Michael. He's now a Christian!" To which he replied, "You just baptized him a Catholic. You have to raise him a Christian."

Having said that, I grew up Catholic with all the accompanying benefits: nuns, priests, the Baltimore catechism, and of course, parochial school. I cruised along just fine until that fateful day when the Beatles came to America. The Fab Four changed our lives inexorably and forever, and my first priority was to grow my hair from a whitewall cut to where at least there wasn't so much white. The end result was still tame by any standard—my hair didn't even touch my collar. Nevertheless, it was long enough to get me kicked out of altar boys.

Due to this and a few other non-hair-raising issues, including my own inclination for new adventures, my parents decided to enroll me in the once-dreaded public school system. In the years to follow, I wasted no time enthusiastically pursuing all the latest trends at an ever-increasing pace: girls, tight pants, Jimi Hendrix, cigarettes, and more girls. Oh yeah, and hair down past my shoulders.

By my senior year, I'd arrived. My girlfriend was everything I'd ever hoped for. She was tall, blond, beautiful, on the pep squad, and she came from a well-off family. A dream come true. Together we dove headlong into everything the counterculture had to offer: alcohol, drugs, music, sex, and underground films.

They were being called "Jesus Freaks." Yeah, great for them. I still needed to make up for lost time.

A minor historical footnote: During this time something else was happening all over the U.S. *Time* magazine reported that burned out, disillusioned hippies were exiting the drug and music culture in droves for, of all things, God. They were being called "Jesus Freaks." Yeah, great for them. I still needed to make up for lost time.

I remember vividly the day my girlfriend was sitting on my lap and looking into my eyes, telling me she wanted to marry me. Sometime in the next few years, I projected, we'd be man and wife. Then after a few more years, we'd raise a family. Somewhere in there I'd graduate from college.

Then one day our perfect world came crashing down when she told me that she was "late." We immediately began to investigate the only option "our" culture had to offer. Terminate the mistake. Keep the deed quiet, sweep it under the rug, and move on.

Time stood still as each tick of the clock brought on increasing dread. Arrangements were made. She would fly to New York and be met by strangers. It would all be over in a matter of hours—like a long sleepover at a friend's house.

The plan was to be implemented at the start of spring break, but instead she abruptly went skiing in Colorado with her family. Silence ensued. Then, almost a week later, I received an enigmatic postcard that read, "An angel of the Lord passed over me, and I'm free," or something like that. Although it didn't sound like her, I knew what she meant. I was prepared for little else. Another friend of hers received a postcard that said she had met the "most amazing man." Mutual friends approached me, surrounding me with long faces and conciliatory remarks. Quietly, to myself, it seemed I'd won the battle but lost the war.

You've got to be kidding me— a Bible!

When she returned, she was a completely different person.

I knew the girl who had left. I knew the weave of her ponytail, the stitch of her jeans, the rhythm of her breathing. The girl who walked through my front door and sat down next to me was a changed person. She was better. She had hope. She was new. And she brought a book.

She excitedly opened up—*you've got to be kidding me*—a Bible! The Bible up until that very moment had been a huge book somewhere in our living room that had stories and a few pictures, but never did I ever imagine that it held things that would affect me, that addressed my condition. Hers was a paperback called *Good News for Modern Man*. She turned to a part in it that she'd underlined and read, "Everyone has sinned and is far away from God's saving presence. But by the free gift of God's grace all are put right with Him through Christ Jesus who sets them free."

Something happened as I listened to her read. She was saying that everyone has messed up. No one is perfect. I felt something coming alive within me. Kicking to get out. I heard—*could it be?*—a voice inside telling me to listen, saying, *This is good stuff. This is about you, Michael.*

When she finished, she asked, "Do you want this? Do you want what I have?"

I asked the only question I could. "Will you still be my girlfriend?"

"No way," she replied. "That's over." At that, she left as quickly as she had arrived.

I felt heartsick, abandoned, even physically ill. My entire world had fallen apart right in front of my eyes within a matter of weeks. Even so, the answer to everything seemed within my grasp. I began a daily, even hourly, debate within myself. *If I do this, I can no longer do this and this and this. And that. Especially that.* But I also thought of the eternal implications. We are here for only about eighty, maybe a hundred years. Compared with eternity, that seemed like a second. Was I willing to give up some things down here for the assurance of doing the right thing for, for…forever?

I now know a story in the Bible about how God physically wrestled with a guy for an entire evening. In the end, He had to break the guy's hip to resolve things. For about a week, I did a very similar exercise with God. It turns out that I was dying to my old self, being reborn.

Ultimately, I went into my brother's empty room (it was the nearest room with a lock on the door) and got down on the floor. I bowed my head, closed my eyes, and prayed. *Dear Jesus, I give up trying to live my life on my own. I want my life to be everything You intended it to be. And in living my life on my own I have sinned, sinned a lot, against You. Please forgive me for these sins.*

When I got up off that indoor/outdoor carpeting, I realized that I had just become a Christian. I had met God. I thought back to those words my grandfather had said to my mother so many years ago, "You have to raise him a Christian." Well, my parents did everything possible to provide a loving, caring Christian home, but there really was no way anyone could make me a Christian. I had to make that choice myself.

The first thing I did was to get into my '67 Volkswagen and rush downtown to tell my best friend what had happened. He was in his apartment listening to the Stones on his stereo. After a few attempts to get his attention, I literally jerked the headphones off his head. Not reacting at first, he listened intently for a few minutes and then said the most remarkable thing. "That happened to me a few years ago, but I didn't have any friends who believed in the same thing."

I was born again for about thirty minutes, and already I'd found a brother! He soon introduced me to another Christian, a high school language instructor, and together we spent the next few months exploring the Scriptures, excitedly finding out what a new life in Christ was all about.

My search was over. I'd finally found the way—the right way— one different from the one my culture promised and shouted from every rooftop but could never fulfill or satisfy.

Michael is a writer/director in Hollywood. His most recent film, *The Ride,* was for World Wide Pictures, the film branch of the Billy Graham Evangelistic Association. He has also directed programs for Charles Colson's Prison Fellowship, the Gospel Association of India, and other Christian organizations. He is an elder in his church and is happily married to his wife, Susan.

28

THE TOUCH OF HIS HAND

Arlene Blanchard

Love is a fruit in season at all times,
and within the reach of every hand.
MOTHER TERESA

A t 9:02 A.M. on April 19, 1995, a bomb blew apart the Murrah Federal Building in Oklahoma City. In that one earth-shattering moment, every event in the twenty-eight years of my life suddenly seemed to converge.

I grew up in the projects of Cleveland, a dismal place for anyone to exist. Oh, life was hard! We were very poor, and many times at the end of the month there was no food to eat. What was the point in living? As a little girl, I would often go outside, look up into the sky at the stars, and wish that I had never been born.

In my younger years, my mother took us to church, where I heard what seemed to be a long list of do's and don'ts about how to get to heaven and how to avoid hell. I was young, and I didn't understand everything they were saying. But I was also ornery and stubborn, and I didn't want to follow all those rules anyway. I wasn't sure if I would make it through life, let alone get to heaven.

Poverty tends to make some people kinder and more appreciative of the things they have and some people more bitter, desperate, and angry. I chose the latter route. I became a very self-centered, mean-spirited person with the attitude "What have you done for me lately?" An acquaintance once said to me, "Arlene, you are so stingy that you wouldn't give a crippled crab a crutch to crawl with." I was proud of that statement. That meant that I was doing my job. Needless to say, I was a loner.

"Arlene, you are so stingy that you wouldn't give a crippled crab a crutch to crawl with."

As a girl, one of my dreams was to be a walking lethal weapon, maybe even an assassin. Living in the projects, surrounded by violence, I never wanted to be in a predicament where I could not defend myself. The military seemed to be my ticket out of Cleveland as well as the place to realize my dream, so as soon as I was old enough, I enlisted in the Army. I would learn how to protect myself *and* get paid for it. Besides, I couldn't afford to go to college or stand the thought of living with my mother any longer.

Joining the Army didn't adjust my attitude. When I was stationed in Italy, my roommate and I were known as the Tag Team Tasmanian Devils. Anything in our path was destined for destruction. We could dice up a person in seconds with our most lethal weapon, the tongue. At that time in my life, I was a party animal, but I didn't drink. I was a control freak, and getting drunk meant that I lost control. Plus, drinking was expensive. It would have taken something pretty extreme to get me, a female Ebenezer Scrooge, to spend some of my hard-earned cash on alcohol.

All that changed when the Army stationed me in Alaska. Although it wasn't as bad as the Cleveland projects, it was a rough place to live. To dull the pain, I soon added drinking to my nightlife. I have an especially vivid memory of that time. It was winter, and people were suffering from cabin fever. It got so bad that we had a couple of suicides on our post. One weekend after drinking and carousing, I took a look in the mirror. Something deep in my eyes caught my attention, and what I saw scared me. I've often heard it said that the eyes are the windows to the soul, and as I was looking into mine, I saw nothing but emptiness and evil. It was one of the most riveting, frightening moments of my life.

Because of the suicides, all personnel had to attend suicide prevention classes given by the post chaplains. Normally, going to a military class meant a chance for a nap. But when that chaplain came to speak to us, I was still shaken up by my look in the mirror, so not only was I awake, I was alert. Something he said got my attention, and I suddenly had the wild notion that I should start going to church.

I had joined the Army in part to escape confrontations with my mother, but in Alaska, as I tried harder and harder to stay in control and keep it together, I discovered that I missed her dearly. To my own surprise, I asked her to come up and live with me. I hadn't thought how hard it would be to party with her there—especially when she happened to be a praying mother. I soon learned that no matter how hard I ran, I couldn't outrun prayer. Shortly after Mom moved in, I actually began to attend church.

As the weeks went on, I learned some things. Growing up, I had been taught that getting to heaven was a matter of following a list of do's and don'ts. But I discovered that being a Christian isn't about rules; it's about a relationship—a relationship with a loving God. I was overwhelmed to realize that God actually loved me, all of me, despite my rebellion, bad attitude, foul mouth, and drinking. In fact, God cared about me so much that He wanted to give me eternal life just for the asking—a free gift! This new information really made me think.

Finally, in a little church on a cold and depressing winter's day in Alaska, I couldn't resist God's love any longer. I gave everything up to Him and invited Jesus Christ to come into my life.

Instantly, I started changing. I watched myself turn into a brand-new person. My heart truly began to soften, and my drinking and partying stopped. I started to have genuine love and compassion for others—me, the former Ms. Ebenezer Scrooge! God even changed my countenance. That mean and hateful girl disappeared.

The rest of my years in the Army brought professional and spiritual growth. I finally left Alaska for more exciting places around the U.S., and I took my growing faith with me. I had a fulfilling career, rich in relationships, joy, and a sense of God's presence wherever I was. In 1994, I married a wonderful man. When the time came for me to leave the Army, I was a completely different person than the wild, angry, hopeless young woman who had enlisted. With God in control, I thought that I could handle anything.

I was about to find out.

April 19, 1995, was the last day of my assignment as an Army personnel sergeant in Oklahoma City. I had just nine days left in the military. I remember that day so vividly. It was such a beautiful morning. I drove to work in my little sports car with the wind blowing through my hair, and instead of taking the elevator, I ran up the stairs to my office on the fourth floor of the Murrah building.

When I arrived at the office, my replacement, Sergeant Tittsworth, had just come in with his wife and his two little girls. I was really looking forward to meeting him because it made my retirement seem all the more real. My supervisor, Sergeant Bennie Evans, was introducing him to everyone in the office, and when he came to me, I blurted out, "Hi! I'm Sergeant Blanchard. Welcome to Oklahoma City!" I think my exuberance scared him.

After the introductions, I went back to my desk to finish up some reports in preparation for my departure. As I was sitting there, Sergeant Tittsworth's three-year-old daughter, Kayla, came over and started talking to me. She was cute, but like most three-year-olds, she quickly got distracted and walked away. I had just turned around to say something to Sergeant Evans, when suddenly what seemed like a ton of bricks hit me in the center of my head and volts of electricity shot up the tips of my toes and coursed through my body and out the top of my head. My entire body was vibrating and shaking. I was plunged into total darkness, and I began screaming at the top of my lungs. Then I passed out.

Suddenly what seemed like a ton of bricks hit me in the center of my head.

When I awoke, I was still in total darkness. I began screaming, "Somebody, please help me! God! Please, somebody help me!" Because I couldn't see, there was no way I could know about the total devastation around me. I couldn't know what in the world had happened and why no one was coming to my aid.

About five minutes later, I regained my sight. I jumped up and tried to run toward the exit. But there was nowhere to go. The entire office had been demolished. Approximately fifteen feet to my left was the opening soon to be known as "the pit." It was the area in front of the building where all nine floors were stacked on top of each other like pancakes. Overcome by confusion and fear, I again began screaming. "Somebody, somebody help me! God, what's going on?"

Then I heard Sergeant Evans. "Sergeant Blanchard, Sergeant Blanchard," he shouted, "calm down!" I knew he was right. In the Army, I had been trained to remain calm in order to define a problem and then move to solve it. But could I handle this?

With arms outstretched to heaven, I cried, "Jesus, my Jesus." I just wanted my Savior to hold my hand. Right then, before I had even finished saying His name, His loving peace covered me like a soft, downy blanket, and immediately I stopped screaming. What I remember most about that day is that Jesus was the first one there to hold my hand.

Sergeant Evans said, "I need you to get seated so I can take roll call." Amid all the rubble and devastation, there was one tiny chair sitting like a little island just waiting for me. When I sat in that chair and looked up, I realized that we were no longer on the fourth floor. There was a crystal clear blue sky with beautiful bright sunlight beaming in from the pit, and I could see billows of black smoke rising from the parking lot where cars were on fire. I listened as Sergeant Evans called the names of my coworkers. Some didn't respond.

I heard the mother of the two little girls screaming, "Kayla, come to Mommy, come to Mommy. Please answer Mommy!" I looked around and saw her across the room, her head covered with blood. As I watched her, I knew that Kayla was never going to answer.

I looked to my left and saw my other supervisor, Captain Lawrence Martin. The blast had propelled him through a wall. He was saturated in blood and clearly in such pain that he couldn't even call for help; he only moaned. I heard another coworker say, "We've got to get a tourniquet on him. We have to stop the bleeding."

Nearby there was another soldier who was able to help me. Master Sergeant Bonebreak came over to me and asked if I could walk. When I replied, "Yes. Yes, I can," he held out his hand and took my hand in his. Never before in my life had I known the importance and power of the human touch. It was Jesus' hand again, but this time in the flesh.

It was Jesus' hand again, but this time in the flesh.

About thirty minutes after the blast, some of my coworkers and I walked out of the building, following the trail of blood left by those who had preceded us. We exited to dazzling sunshine and the cheers of rescuers and other survivors just waiting to see who else would walk out the door. What a stark contrast to the dark recesses of the standing rubble I had just left!

The smiling faces were a sight to behold. They were angels there to meet me. That's when I found out the building had been bombed.

Jesus' faithfulness and compassion didn't end on April 19. He held my hand through the many painful days that followed. When I attended church the first Sunday after the bombing, God gave me a small revelation, a glimmer of hope for the future. As I walked into the sanctuary, I saw Romans 8:28 displayed on the screen: "And we know that in all things God works for the good of those who love him, who have been called according to his purpose." This verse resonated within me as never before, and even though I could not then see how anything good could come from something so evil, I clung to this promise from God.

The horror of living through that bombing was earthshaking. The pain, anger, and anguish of that diabolical incident seemed to surge through every cell in my body. The whirlwind of emotions within me caused stomach ulcers, chronic migraines, and many sleepless nights. My appearance became stark. At twenty-eight, I could have passed for Methuselah's grandmother.

In my own power, I never could have overcome my grief or forgiven the individuals responsible for that unspeakable tragedy. The bomb killed 171 people and blew apart the lives of hundreds of others. Some survivors even committed suicide because they couldn't handle the emotional trauma. But with God's strength, I was able to squelch the raging monster of unforgivingness within. The gentle whispers of His still, small voice soothed my soul.

God has said that He makes all the things that happen to His children work together for good. I am a living witness to the truth of that statement. God turned this tragedy into a triumphant work as He allowed me to share with others His awesome power and love and to pass on the hope that I now have.

Where would I be if I had not yielded to God years earlier? If He had not taken away my bitterness and self-pity, I know I would never have survived.

Since retiring from the Army, Arlene has been an aerobics instructor and a securities/life insurance agent. She and her husband, Stan, have two young sons, Hunter and Lawton. After the bombing, Arlene founded The Cross and the Dove, a ministry to help people triumph through tragedy in their lives. The name of the ministry comes from a photo taken of the building where Arlene was sitting at the time of the blast. Sunlight beaming down on the rubble in the building created an image of a cross and a dove. Arlene's e-mail address is albblessed@juno.com.

29

CHANGED FROM THE INSIDE OUT

Michael Miller

*If you take a drink, then the drink takes a drink,
then the drink takes you.*
F. SCOTT FITZGERALD

At the age of twenty-three, I was a drug addict. In 1982, for the fourth year in a row, my New Year's resolution was to get off drugs. That year my commitment to abstinence lasted less than two days.

I had started experimenting with marijuana six years earlier, and I quickly went on to more potent, even life-threatening, drugs. I tried it all—LSD, hashish, pills, PCP, and other drugs that fry the brain.

In my early teens it had been easy to say no when friends offered me drugs. I had a good life, and I had seen enough antidrug films in elementary school to know that drugs would ruin it. Besides, drums were my high. There's no doubt I was born to be a drummer. While I was still very young, my mother gave me a pair of drumsticks to keep the prints of my pounding fingers off the furniture, and when I was thirteen, my father gave me a drum set of my own. In high school, drums even took first place over girlfriends.

Well, almost…. I have to admit that I was head over heels in puppy love with my first girlfriend. By my senior year, I was day-dreaming that we'd get married someday and raise a family. As I pictured my future kids, I wondered what I'd do if they got caught smoking pot. It occurred to me that it would be hypocritical of me to tell them to say no to drugs if I had never tried them myself. That one thought led to my downfall.

Shortly thereafter I asked some friends who used drugs if I could try smoking some pot. They were happy to let me try. I didn't see colors, hallucinate, or get sick, as I always thought I would. As a matter of fact, I really didn't feel anything. My friends assured me that I would have to smoke it a few times before I'd feel something.

One day after I had smoked marijuana a few more times, I started playing my drums. It sure seemed to me that I was playing better than I ever had. They came alive under my sticks! That convinced me that pot was a good thing and—for the sake of my music—I smoked more. It wasn't long before my taste in music changed from the top ten hits to heavy metal, and soon I was deep into the dark side of the music world.

It was easy to start experimenting with other drugs because drumming in a heavy metal band brought lots of them my way. Angel dust—the street name for PCP—is a powerful drug that people smoke to get a heroin-like high. I knew that it fries a brain quicker than anything else around, but I didn't care. My goal was to be a better drummer.

Instead, I quickly found that it slurred my speech and screwed up my motor skills. I noticed that my right foot, which plays the bass drum, didn't respond the way it used to. Even though I was taking all different kinds of drugs, it was easy to pinpoint the cause of my problems. Playing the drums was the most important thing in my life, and I knew that I had to stop messing with PCP. It took a few weeks to wean myself, but amazingly, I was able to kick the habit. However, I was still addicted to high-end marijuana and cocaine. I considered them lightweight compared to PCP, and they didn't hurt my drumming. So I thought, *No harm done.*

For a few years life seemed good as I tried for higher highs in a life in the fast lane. My rock 'n' roll friends gave me a lot of free drugs to "keep me happy." "You always want to keep your drummer happy!" they'd say. Yet, the free drugs were never enough. To afford my growing daily habit, I began to deal drugs. Soon that became my main income. I lived with my parents, which also helped financially, but I had to become good at hiding my addiction from them if I wanted to continue living there. In order not to get busted when I got home, I used Visine to "get the red out" and tried to walk straight when I came through the door. As long as I could do that, my secret was safe.

Once I even threw a girl across the room. I was becoming a monster.

For a long time I was blind to the mood-altering effect the drugs had on me. I went through many girlfriends, even having several at the same time. Still, I became paranoid when I suspected any of them of two-timing me. If I even thought that one of them was involved with another guy, I would fly into a jealous rage. Once I even threw a girl across the room. I was becoming a monster.

By the time I was twenty, I needed more and more money to support my drug habit. Somehow, I was able to land a job at the Los Angeles headquarters of a large California bank. Even when I was high, I functioned well enough to hold on to my job, so I regularly got loaded on breaks and during the lunch hour. But as I got to know the people I worked with, I noticed that without the need for drugs, they seemed so free, so peaceful, and so "normal" that I wanted to be like them. Yet I couldn't. Maybe it was too late.

Two years later I was still wishing I could be straight like the nice people I worked with. Once again I tried to get off the drugs, but to no avail. Although I thought I was in control, I obviously wasn't, for I couldn't shake off the physical addiction that by then was the driving force of my existence.

Then one day a friend invited me to a series of free rock concerts at some church. At the first two, I went out to the parking lot to get high during intermission and before I went home. My constant need had me sneaking around a church, avoiding anyone who might see, in order to get my quick high.

At the third concert, however, I was able to listen to a few of the songs and hear what the pastor said right after the concert. Certain words stuck, but there was one sentence that pounded in my head: "Jesus will change you from the inside out." That's what the pastor kept saying to us that night. Was that possible? Could I really change and actually become like my friends at work?

Who had touched me? That touch was so real.

Right at that moment, I felt the lightest touch of a gentle hand over my heart. *What was that?* I looked to my right and left and even turned around, but there was no one near me with an outstretched arm. *Who had touched me?* That touch was so real.

When the pastor invited people to stay after, I responded. But as I followed the people who wanted to talk with me about God, I was very much on guard, fearing that this might just be some crazy cult trying to kidnap and brainwash me. I was prepared to turn over some chairs if they tried to get me. But I quickly realized that there was nothing to fear. They were sincere, kind people who never asked me for money or tried to force anything down my throat or draw me into their church. They even told me to go find a church that I was comfortable with and to read the Bible to find out about Jesus for myself. Then someone prayed with me. I was scared about what would happen, but I knew that submitting my whole life to Jesus was the right thing to do.

That's when the miracle happened. Right there, as sure as I'm writing about it today, Jesus made Himself real to me and removed my drug addiction. That was the night I met God. I went home a new person, healed of a habit that had controlled every day of my life for six years. In answer to one heartfelt prayer, God just took it away. The power of that moment suddenly gave me a new longing for a relationship with Him. I will never forget it for as long as I live.

Two weeks later, I was talking with an old friend from my drug days. As we talked, I became upset with his vulgar language. He said the *f* word with every breath, and it really bugged me. Then it hit me. I had been known for having the worst mouth of all my friends. Every sentence that came out had a string of foul words in it. But since that prayer at the church, I hadn't said one single swear word. I couldn't believe it. Jesus had already started changing me from the inside out, just as that pastor had said He would. And that wasn't all. He also started changing things that I didn't even know needed changing.

Almost immediately my parents moved to a new neighborhood a few miles away, which allowed me to make new friends and walk away from the old ones. I soon met a wonderful girl who accepted my past and embraced my miraculous change. I had the honor of telling her about Jesus, and He changed her life too.

We married two years later and now have three lovely children. I'm happily working for California's largest HMO as one of those normal people in corporate America, and every Monday on my lunch hour I lead a Bible study. I attend a great church, I've developed some incredible Christian friendships, and I'm constantly learning more about God and how much He cares about me. Drugs haven't tempted me for so many years that I sometimes wonder why I had to literally fry my brain before I came to know real freedom.

It's been twenty years since I've picked up the drumsticks, but I have a new passion in life. Once a month, I go to Juvenile Hall to speak to the kids there and help the ones who are addicted to drugs. What an amazing miracle it is to have them come up to me and pour out their lives, their struggles, and their addictions. As I tell them about the hope, the new beginning, and the freedom that Jesus gave me, I see the life of one child after another transformed—all because of God's life-changing message of love. He really does change us from the inside out!

Michael is a third-generation Californian who enjoys working as a network administrator for Kaiser Permanente in Pasadena. His best times are spent with his three wonderful kids. He also runs in 5K races, rides his bike enthusiastically, and even finds time to run his own side business of personal computer repair and consulting. You can visit him at michaeljamesmiller@yahoo.com.

FREE FALL

Michael

Most people would succeed in small things,
if they were not troubled by great ambitions.
HENRY WADSWORTH LONGFELLOW

F ree fall, rushing toward the rocks below—that describes the state I was in when I was twenty-six years old. On the outside, I was outgoing and popular; but on the inside, I was extremely shy and desperately searching for meaning.

I was born in Chicago. Neither of my parents talked about God much, though we went to church during my early years because it was the thing to do. My home life was very volatile. I remember my parents fighting constantly. They divorced when I was four, and several years later my father was tragically killed. I never had a real chance to know my father, and yet his death left a gaping hole in my life.

Afraid of raising two boys on her own, Mom quickly remarried, and my brother and I spent the remainder of our childhood moving all over the Midwest as my stepfather transferred from one Fortune 500 company to another. It was an extremely painful experience for me to be ripped constantly from friends I had just made, only to have to start all over again. The hardest move was in the middle of my freshman year of high school. I had made a lot of friends in Chicago, and then we up and moved to Boston. Out of frustration and fear that we'd just move again, I refused to really connect with anyone.

When it came time to go to college, I was determined to get as far away from Boston as I could, so I chose Tulane University in New Orleans, where I pursued a degree in business. For me, college life equaled party life. I studied and did quite well academically during the week, but I was even better at partying on the weekend. I experimented with various drugs and drank a lot. It was the late seventies, and everyone else was doing it, so it didn't seem like a big deal.

After I graduated, I moved to Lahaina, Maui, to clear my head and vacation for a while before I settled into a boring job as a businessman. There, I looked to nature to find the answer to my spiritual emptiness. I knew that there had to be an awesome Creator for there to be so much beauty in nature, so I read a lot of Emerson and Thoreau and became intimately connected with creation by getting absorbed in the amazing Hawaiian sunsets. I had never gotten over losing my father, so I talked to "God" often; but a deep longing for someone more tangible haunted me.

About that time, I met a man who was vacationing in Maui. I was making my living waiting tables, and this man and his family had sat at one of my tables repeatedly over the course of a week. One night I noticed that he kept staring at me, so I finally asked why he took such an interest. He said that God had put a tremendous burden on his heart for me. He introduced himself as Jack, said that he was a pastor from San Jose, California, and asked if there was anything he could do for me. I didn't know what to say. He then asked if he could keep in touch with me and told me that he'd be praying for me. It didn't freak me out or anything. I just could have taken it or left it. So I gave him my phone number and address, expecting that to be the end of it.

Shortly thereafter, my restaurant career took off, and I ended up managing Chart House restaurants in La Jolla, California; Lahaina, Maui; and Sun Valley, Idaho. My life was about hard work, making money, partying, and having fun.

For years, Jack sent me letters with verses from the Bible about God and how much God loved me. I was very touched, especially since, having kept my stepfather at arm's length my entire life, I didn't really have a father figure with whom I could share my inner turmoil. And yet, I still didn't have my act together. Although I had not yet learned to recognize God, I had started to sense that there was a parachute on my back ready to rescue me from my unending free fall. I began to hold out hope.

> *I had started to sense that there was a parachute on my back ready to rescue me from my unending free fall.*

In late 1984, I decided that it was time to put my degree to work. It was the eighties: Reagan was in the White House, and money was flowing. Wall Street intrigued me, especially the oil returns. So on a whim, I gave up the restaurant world and moved to Dallas to get into the oil business.

By 1985, I had by far surpassed my income managing restaurants and was thoroughly enjoying my work. But I was also living in the fast lane. I worked compulsively hard during the week at my business and kept my body in shape by hitting the gym twice a day. It looked like a clean life Monday through Friday, but when the weekends came, I would drop off the face of the earth into drugs and alcohol. I was caught up in an obsessive lifestyle, full of illicit sex, partying, and very little sleep. I was lost and knew it, but I couldn't get out. Meanwhile, I kept calling out to "God"—whoever he was.

In January 1986, Jack came to Dallas for a conference. We had dinner, and I was honest with him about my life, including all the partying. He asked if I wanted a relationship with God. I said, "Well…yeah…that's what I've been searching for my entire life." We went to his hotel, where four other ministers joined us. That night, I prayed with them to ask Jesus to come into my heart and take over my life. That was the day I met God.

But when I left, I didn't feel anything magical inside, so I wasn't sure if I had done it just because of pressure from all those minis-

What happened next will forever play in slow motion in my mind.

ters. Although I figured that it might not have been real, at least now I had someone to direct my prayers to. I began praying directly to Jesus instead of to a generic god.

My weekend behavior was not quick to change. I continued my Dr. Jeckyl-and-Mr. Hyde existence. But as time went by, I slowly became aware that I was responsible for my own discontent. I realized that my actions were what were keeping me running on empty.

Then, one leisurely weekend several months later, I got a wake-up call that changed my life drastically. I had gone waterskiing to clear my head. At the end of a full, energized day of skiing, I was at the end of the boat reeling in the ski rope. For whatever reason, my friend driving the boat was edgy, and as I was pulling in the rope and wrapping it around my arm, he gunned the boat without warning me. What happened next will forever play in slow motion in my mind. The moment the boat sped off, the rope made a tourniquet around my arm just above the bicep.

I remember being dragged underwater and feeling this tremendous pull on my arm. My body was acting like a resistance. The boat was in full throttle, and the rope dragged me through the water for about thirty seconds before my friends noticed that I was missing. I blacked out, and when I awoke, still in the water, I felt excruciating pain at the top of my left arm.

The next thing I knew, I was hanging on the boat with my good arm, looking down at my injured arm, which was flapping around like a fish out of water. The rope had cut through my bicep and triceps, severed the nerve, and crushed the arteries. There was no feeling in the arm, and it looked like it was about to fall off.

I panicked. I felt a horrible fear that I might lose my arm. Then, as quickly as the fear came upon me, it gave way to a tremendous, inexplicable peace. I just knew that I was going to survive. Becoming very calm, I was able to tell the guys in the boat what to do.

Mysteriously, one of them found a knife in his bag that had not been there before. It was sharp enough to cut through the nylon ski rope. I was rushed to a hospital in Ft. Worth and then quickly transferred to a hospital in Dallas. During a long and complicated operation, a vascular surgeon took arteries from my legs to replace those that had been severed in my arm. I was in the hospital for two weeks. Miraculously, I came out with two working arms.

When I had accepted Jesus into my life six months earlier, I hadn't even been sure that He had listened. Now it all became clear. God had been there all along, drawing me toward Him, even when I had continued to live a wild lifestyle. And in a life-and-death situation when I needed Him most, He had unmistakably revealed Himself.

The peace that engulfed me had nothing to do with me; it was clearly from God. At that moment I finally learned that I truly had met God and that Jesus truly was my Savior. It was a real, physical event that changed my life.

I knew without a doubt that it was time to clean up my act and change the way I was living. I wanted a complete change—spiritually, mentally, and physically. My mom and stepfather had begun a personal relationship with God years before, and now I realized that they had been praying for me all along. God clearly used my mother in my life. As I grew in my relationship with Jesus, I realized that He had a plan for my life that was slowly but surely being revealed.

God—the real God—got my attention first through Reverend Jack in Maui and then during that horrible water-skiing accident in Texas. Although it has not always been an easy road since then, my search for meaning ended fifteen years ago. Throughout my ups and downs in life, God is always there, tugging at my heart and watching over me. No matter what new trial comes my way, I know that I'm no longer in a free fall, for God has me firmly in His grip.

Michael has been an agent in the entertainment industry since 1990. Currently he is a literary agent in Beverly Hills, California, where he represents award-winning television/feature writers, producers, and directors. He's actively involved in the ministries of Premise and MasterMedia. He is happily married and the father of two wonderful children.

31

THE JOURNEY OF A LIFETIME

Cathy L. Chang

The world is a book, and those who do not travel read only one page.
ST. AUGUSTINE

What a summer it was—the summer of 1999. I spent it riding my bicycle across the United States from Los Angeles to Boston. I had taken a leave of absence from my job as a transportation consultant with a large engineering firm, and my husband, Glen, although he was not enamored with the idea, supported me in this adventure. So, on a bright sunny day in May, I stood ankle-deep in the Pacific Ocean, ready to embark on the journey of a lifetime.

The bike trip from coast to coast took seven weeks. For forty-nine days, our group of forty-two riders biked eighty miles a day through the traffic of Los Angeles, the heat of the desert, the endless prairies of Kansas, the roller-coaster hills of Missouri, the cornfields of Illinois, and the forests of upstate New York. Continually on the lookout for that perfect potty bush, we had a new bed every night, mediocre buffet food for breakfast and dinner, and sports drinks and energy gels for lunch.

Being a private person and slow to make lasting friends, I spent much of the trip riding alone, mesmerized by the countryside and not thinking about anything in particular. I was not on the trip to achieve an emotional breakthrough, reevaluate my life, or consider changing my career, marital status, or anything else. My only agenda was to ride my bike, have fun, and enjoy the summer. And that's exactly what I did.

After riding 3,429 miles, we arrived at Boston on July 2. The entire group rode those last five miles together, two by two, side by side, friends with friends. Forty-two strangers had met in Los Angeles seven weeks ago. Now, forty-one lifelong friends rode together to Revere Beach and stared in awe at the Atlantic Ocean. We had done it! We had accomplished our goal—we had ridden our bikes completely across this great country of ours. Our incredibly exciting, sometimes treacherous, adventure had forged a bond among us. We would never be the same—especially me!

As we got off our bikes, we knew it was time to say a farewell. Emotions were running high. We had just spent seven weeks laughing together, crying together, and becoming part of one another's lives. We were there to help fulfill one another's dreams, to pick one another up (sometimes literally), and even to mourn the death of one of our riders along the way. We had supported, encouraged, and cheered one another across the country. Now, here we were on the last day of our adventure. I was going to miss my dear new friends.

As we were standing on this beautiful beach, crying and hugging, Bob called me over to his bike and said that he had something for me. All the way across the country I had watched a yellow necktie flutter behind his bike, hanging off his bike bag. Now he carefully and ceremoniously cut off a piece of it, handed it to me, and said, "Jesus loves you and so do I." The tie had little happy faces surrounded by tiny lettering that said, "Jesus loves you." I appreciated the gift and thanked Bob for it. But truthfully,

I didn't give it much thought at the time. I was too preoccupied with saying good-bye, and I had no clue who Jesus was.

On the plane ride back to California, however, I started thinking about what Bob had said and about the yellow tie with the little smiley faces. I took it out and stared at it. For some reason, the message seemed to be for me, but I couldn't figure out why. I was sitting next to Ed, another rider from our trip. We were sharing our feelings about it, and I mentioned the tie and how I felt about its message. Ed said that he thought God might be trying to talk to me. *I don't know,* I thought, *I don't even believe in God.* He then asked if he could pray for me, which he did. I thought that I wasn't feeling much of anything until suddenly I started to cry. Ed was praying, I was crying, and I'm sure that the guy sitting next to us couldn't figure out what was going on.

Ed was praying, I was crying, and I'm sure that the guy sitting next to us couldn't figure out what was going on.

Ed and I changed planes in Denver. Still in tears, I said good-bye to him and called Glen from a phone booth. When he asked what was wrong, I said, "I'm not sure, but I think that God might exist. We have to go to church tomorrow." Needless to say, Glen was quite surprised.

Seven weeks earlier, I had left home an atheist or agnostic—I'm not even sure which. I might have believed in some generic supreme being, but I had no idea who or what it was. I didn't need any organized religion or belief system. I was superwoman. I could do anything and everything I wanted to. I didn't need any "life answers," because I already had them all. I was in charge of my own life and doing rather well at it—or so I thought. Work was my number one priority. After that came biking. That was all I needed. I had no interest in religion, spirituality, or in adding any other dimension to my life. I had kept religion out of my friendships because it just wasn't anything I felt I needed to discuss with anyone. It just wasn't a part of my life.

But now the events of the bike trip sparked something in the deep recesses of my mind. It was just enough to make me wonder about things. I felt that if there was a possibility that something was out there, I had to investigate. Suddenly, I went from being antireligious to being inquisitive—to asking, "Hey, what else is out there?" Over the next few weeks, I started asking others what they believed in and why. I had endless questions. I called Bob, and he became my spiritual mentor on my new journey. I often lunched with a friend at work so I could grill him on Christianity and what it meant. But it seemed that the more questions I asked, the more I had.

I started going to church, and I began reading the Bible and other books on Christianity. I read anything I could get my hands on—one book at night, another during my lunch breaks, and one any free moment in between. I asked even more questions, beginning with "Why would God want to talk to me?" As I talked with my friends about this, I realized that some of them had a strong faith, while others just professed to believe. Some people did not understand what it meant to be a Christian. Others, like the old me, simply did not want to hear anything about Him.

The next few months were filled with incredible "coincidences" as things just seemed to fall into place. I reconnected with a high school girlfriend who *just happened* to be going through the same search that I was. I found an Alpha class on the fundamentals of the Christian faith that *just happened* to meet on my free evenings. I found a church that *just happened* to be on my bike route. And the pastor *just happened* to bike. I developed new friendships, asked more questions, and continued to read both the Bible and other recommended books. Once I started reading a book, I could not put it down. Something grabbed my attention and kept me focused on—even obsessed with—this God.

When I came home from my second Alpha class, I found a

package from Bob on my doorstep. He and his wife had sent me a book titled *The Gift for all People: Thoughts on God's Great Grace*. I read it in two nights and pondered what it said: God has given us a wonderful gift—the gift of a Savior and eternal salvation. Jesus Christ was sent here so that we can have a relationship with God—so that we can experience God's love and know His plan for our life. That was a revelation to me, and it left me feeling very unsettled. At that time, I was also reading *Basic Christianity*. In both books, I had come to the place where they were asking me to make a decision. I spoke to Bob, and he said, "You are in the midst of making the most important decision of your life. Are you going to follow Jesus, or not?" Somehow, I already knew what my answer was.

> *He was reaching out to me again, but instead of gently knocking on the door, He was pounding on it!*

That next day was Friday. I went to work, but I was totally dysfunctional. I sat there at my computer just staring out the window, unable to concentrate on anything. Dealing with these new thoughts drained all my mental, emotional, and physical energy. Although I knew that I had options, something in the back of my mind told me that my decision was inevitable—that somehow I had already decided to accept Jesus and that now I just had to acknowledge my decision consciously and implement it publicly.

I was actually believing this! That was pretty amazing to me—me, who three months earlier would have brushed this aside with a quick sweep of the hand; me, who for the first thirty-seven years of my life hadn't paid any attention at all to the patient, benevolent, friendly God who wanted to talk to me. Now, He was reaching out to me again, but instead of gently knocking on the door, He was pounding on it! He took me by the hand and showed me the way. He made things happen that I needed to see. And, at last, He had become real to me.

I went back to work Saturday to try to make up for the Friday I had wasted, but to no avail. I still couldn't concentrate on anything else. All I could think of was that God wanted me to love Him and that I couldn't ignore Him anymore. I finally decided that now was the time to implement my decision.

The day I met God was Saturday, October 9, 1999, at 5:50 in the evening. I received the greatest gift of all, the gift of a lifetime—the gift of eternal salvation. I felt what I can only describe as an inner happiness deep down inside my soul. My view of the world was already changing, and I had a peace and a joy that others recognized immediately.

But something was still bothering me—Glen was not a believer. Our lives had revolved around work and biking and not much else. Our marriage was fine, but nothing terribly exciting. For many years we had just sort of existed together. Now I wanted more. I wanted my husband to have the joy and peace that I had experienced.

From the day I had called him from the airport, Glen had supported my spiritual journey, just as he had supported my biking adventure. Although he wanted to make sure that I wasn't getting involved in some cult or being manipulated by mind games, he was very open-minded about my discoveries. He attended church with me regularly and gave me time alone to think, read, and take the Alpha class. He didn't go to the first Alpha session with me because he felt that this was my own personal journey, but with some gentle encouragement and the prayers of many people, including friends and relatives around the country, he signed up for the next one. Seven months later, on May 10, 2000, Glen also accepted Christ's gift of salvation.

Since then, things have only gotten better. There is a richness and fullness to our marriage that wasn't there before. My relationships with others are also stronger and deeper. Deep down inside, I have a joy that I have never felt before. I still have the same job, but I approach it differently. It's the same me, but I feel differently.

And the only thing that can explain the difference is that Jesus is now a part of my life.

I will never forget the summer of '99. I experienced the journey of my dreams—the journey of a lifetime. But more importantly, I began a journey of faith in Jesus Christ, and I will live the rest of my days knowing that God will be with me forever.

Cathy and Glen live in the San Francisco Bay area and worship at First Presbyterian Church in San Mateo, where they continue to be involved in the Alpha program. She is still employed by the company that generously gave her the summer off and is now planning a bike trip down the West Coast. Cathy is thankful for the many people who brought both her and Glen to know the Lord and who have touched their lives in a special way.

32

THE CHOSEN CHILD

Dr. Robert Petterson

God asks no man whether he will accept life.
That is not the choice. One must take it. The only choice is how.
HENRY WARD BEECHER

Unloved at home, she looked for love in all the wrong places. At fifteen she became pregnant and, abandoned by her family, wandered the streets until she found her way to a home for unwed mothers. On May 19, 1947, she gave birth to a baby boy. I was that unwanted child.

One night my mother slipped away, abandoning me to the care of the state. A few weeks later she married a young man she had picked up in a bar. They came back, retrieved me, and headed west.

My mother's young husband was in the Air Force, and he spent most of the next six years on tours of duty overseas. Lonely and unfulfilled, she spent her nights in the taverns, still looking for love in all the wrong places. She gave birth to five more children, and as the oldest, it fell to me to care for them.

My mother was often away for days at a time. Before she left, she would fix a pan of fried cornmeal mush. After that ran out, we would eat ketchup sandwiches or whatever else we could scrounge from the cupboards. All of us slept in one bed on filthy sheets soaked with urine.

As bad as it was when our mother was gone, it was worse when she came home. Often she brought men from the tavern. Some of them verbally or physically abused us. A few of them sexually molested me. I felt abandoned and lonely, but I also felt an overwhelming sense of responsibility for holding my family together. It was an awesome burden for such a young boy to bear.

It was an awesome burden for such a young boy to bear.

Then came the catastrophic day when my mother's husband came home from a tour of duty. The apartment was in shambles. We were half-naked and unfed. In a fit of rage, he began to beat her, and she ran from the house. Later the police came. They parceled us out in pairs to my mother's friends from the tavern, and a bitter divorce and custody battle ensued. I never lived with my mother or her husband again.

My first foster parents were both alcoholics, and their home was wracked with violence. He often beat me during his drunken fits, but more often he abused her. One night in a drunken rage, he beat her to death with a hammer.

We were quickly taken from that home and made wards of the state. For five years we were shuffled frequently from house to house. In one house they treated us like animals, punishing us by making us eat out of dog dishes. I was nine years old at the time and still wet the bed. The woman decided that she could break me of the habit by treating me like a puppy. She made me kneel by the bed and then rubbed my face in the urinated sheets. When that didn't work, she showed the sheets to my friends and schoolmates, but her attempts to shame me failed to break me of wetting the bed.

Every night at bedtime I would fervently pray, *God, please don't let me wet the bed again.* Every morning the sheets would be wet. I would pull the covers over the sheets and tell my foster mother that I hadn't wet the bed. At night, I would climb back into bed, the sheets still damp and reeking of rancid urine, for another miserable night of fear and self-loathing.

When I was twelve, the experts declared that I had the sociability of a four-year-old. One of my schoolteachers wrote, "This boy needs to be institutionalized. He will never amount to anything." We had passed through so many homes that I had never figured out who—or whose—I was. More than anything, I wanted a family and a name.

Though I hated Him, God never stopped loving me.

One summer for one magnificent month, all six of us children were together in the same neighborhood. It was the happiest time of my life. Then my two brothers were adopted. On the cruel day that their new parents took them away to Florida, I chased the car down the gravel road, screaming with all my might, "Don't go. Please, dear God, don't let them go." I'll never forget the tear-stained faces of my brothers, pressed up against the rear window, as the car sped off into the distance. It was the last time I ever saw them.

I ran to the potato field behind our foster home. Burying my face in the dirt, I wept until I could weep no more. When I got up, I turned my mud-caked face to the sky, shook my fist, and screamed, "God, if You are there, I hate You. I hate You." I had been abandoned too many times.

Though I hated Him, God never stopped loving me.

Across the state lived a childless couple. Arnold was a successful commercial fisherman. His wife, Mary, was desperate for a child. Unable to have children of her own and considered too old to adopt a baby, she went to the state welfare department. The authorities warned her that the only available children were older boys and girls from broken homes. These kids were damaged goods, they said. Adopting any of them was risky business.

But Mary would not be deterred. She wanted a son. They brought her a book filled with the photographs of abandoned children—all wards of the state—and my picture was there. When she saw it among all the others, she said quietly and firmly, "That's the boy I want!"

I'll never forget the day Arnold and Mary Petterson came to our foster home. It was at Christmas time in 1959, and I was twelve years old. I stood shivering in the cold on the front porch, a new pair of shoes pinching my feet. I knew that they had come to check me out and that if they liked me, they just might adopt me. It was the most terrifying moment of my life. I desperately wanted a real family, but I was so sure that they would never choose me.

I was sure that if I bowled a couple of strikes, they would like me enough to adopt me.

Then an amazing thing happened. Mary leaped from the car, ran up the sidewalk, pulled me off the porch, encased me in a breathtaking hug, and declared, "Bobby, I love you." No one had ever said "I love you" to me before. It was a moment of delicious ecstasy. More than forty years later, I still get a lump in my throat when I remember that moment.

That afternoon, Arnold and Mary took me bowling. I was sure that if I bowled a couple of strikes, they would like me enough to adopt me. To my dismay, I bowled a string of gutter balls. I was devastated. Who would want a kid who couldn't even knock down a single bowling pin?

Later they took me to a Chinese restaurant. My spirits perked up when I came up with a foolproof plan to redeem the debacle at the bowling alley: I would eat my meal with chopsticks. Surely they would love a kid who could handle chopsticks! To my utter horror, the sticks got tangled up, and I shot a wad of chow mein across the table into Arnold's lap. I was ruined!

But Arnold smiled at me. Deftly flicking the noodles from his lap, he reached under the table and brought out a hand-carved model of his fishing boat. Tears welled up in Mary's eyes. That was their prearranged signal: If Arnold wanted to adopt me, he would give me the boat. Then Arnold asked the question that has never ceased to make me feel humble and grateful: "Bobby, would you like to be our son and become part of our family?" Would I!

A few days later I joined my new family. The first day I went to my new school, some of my classmates taunted me: "You aren't a real kid. Our parents had us the normal way, but you're just an adopted kid." I was heartbroken.

That night, Mary ran her fingers through my hair and soothed my fears. "Bobby," she said, "the rest of those parents had to take what they got from the hospital. But you're extra special. We picked you out of all the children in the world and chose you to belong to us. And chosen children are the most precious ones in the whole world."

Those words were medicine for a wounded soul.

That night I didn't wet the bed. I could scarcely contain the joy and relief I felt when I awakened in a warm and dry bed for the first time in my life. A lifetime of healing was beginning, and the best was yet to come.

During the turbulent sixties, I attended Seattle Pacific University, and one evening while I was a student there, I attended a meeting of Campus Crusade for Christ. The speaker seemed to look directly at me as he spoke of the *aloneness* of a soul apart from God. He talked about hippies—the disenfranchised young people who were joining communes in a desperate search for family. Then he talked about the Father who was searching for lost children to adopt into His eternal family.

I remember his words: "There is someone very special here tonight. Out of all the people in the world, God has chosen you to become a part of His family." Then he talked about the incredible love of this heavenly Father, who had paid the ultimate price by sacrificing His one and only Son to purchase His lost children.

I remembered how Arnold and Mary Petterson had chosen me from among all the photographs in the book of abandoned children. I recalled the incredible price they had paid by investing their lives in me when I had nothing to offer in exchange. I couldn't even bowl or use chopsticks!

Hadn't God done the same—and so much more—for me? He chose me even though I had nothing to offer Him. I would never have to perform in order to earn or keep His love. He loved me even though I had told Him that I hated Him. As special as I was to the Pettersons, I was infinitely more so to God. The Petterson family wouldn't be permanent, and no earthly relationship is ultimately secure, but my heavenly Father would never abandon me, and the family of God would be with me forever. God would never love me any more or any less than He did when He first found me as a lost and broken sinner.

That night I became part of God's family by committing my life to Jesus Christ.

I feel no resentment toward my birth mother. She could have taken the easy way out and had an abortion. Instead, she chose to give birth to me, and when she was incapable of caring for me, she gave me up for adoption. I no longer feel bitterness toward the people or circumstances that made my childhood so traumatic. Instead, I see that those painful experiences gave me a sensitivity that has prepared me for a unique ministry in the lives of countless people around the world.

I no longer feel the despair that I once felt at the loss of my birth family—my five brothers and sisters. Instead, I delight in my countless brothers and sisters in Christ. A few years ago, dear Mary Petterson died, and one day Arnold will join her. Sometimes these losses make me sad, but I've learned that no human family is permanent. The only lasting love is from the Father who chose me to be His child forever.

> How great is the love the Father has lavished on us, that we should be called children of God! And that is what we are!... Dear friends, now we are children of God, and what we will be has not yet been made known. But we know that when he appears, we shall be like him, for we shall see him as he is. (1 John 3:1–2)

I don't know what is yet in store for me, but I am certain of this: The best is still to come.

D r. Petterson is the East Coast president of Mastermedia International, which ministers to the personal needs of professionals in the entertainment industry. He was senior pastor of Christ Presbyterian Church in Tulsa, Oklahoma, for nineteen years and in Houston, Texas, for eight years. He is an adjunct professor at Covenant Theological Seminary in St. Louis and is listed in *Who's Who in American Colleges and Universities* and *Outstanding Young Men in America*. He has been married to Joyce for thirty-two years and is the father of Rachael Elizabeth, a college senior.

WE WANT TO HEAR FROM YOU

We would love to receive your personal story of how you met God.

We're looking for stories of how your life changed when you met God or how He got you through impossible situations. Telling others how God has personally and powerfully transformed your life could touch the hearts of thousands of searching and discouraged people.

If you write out a short story (2,500 words or less) and send it to us, we'll consider it for future volumes. Or you could pass this on to a friend whose personal story has touched you in some way. For more information or to submit your story, please e-mail us or contact us at the address below.

No Freaking Out!
P.O. Box 433
North Hollywood, CA 91603
E-mail: nofreakingout@aol.com
Web site: www.thrillinglife.com

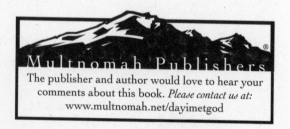

The publisher and author would love to hear your comments about this book. *Please contact us at:*
www.multnomah.net/dayimetgod

Push Fear Aside and Start Sharing Jesus with Confidence!

ISBN 1-57673-737-3

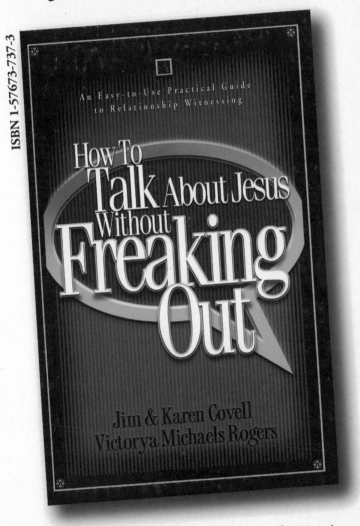

An Easy-to-Use Practical Guide
to Relationship Witnessing

How To Talk About Jesus Without Freaking Out

Jim & Karen Covell
Victorya Michaels Rogers

"Jim, Karen, and Victorya are in the front lines of spiritual influence. This book is a must read."
—Bill Bright

"This book is practical, challenging, and compelling."
—Josh McDowell